The CAD Design Studio

3D Modeling as a Fundamental Design Skill

Stephen Paul Jacobs
Professor
School of Architecture
Tulane University

Models and Illustrations
with the assistance
of
David Pedersen

McGraw-Hill, Inc.
New York St. Louis San Francisco Auckland Bogotá
Caracas Hamburg Lisbon London Madrid
Mexico Milan Montreal New Delhi Paris
San Juan São Paulo Singapore
Sydney Tokyo Toronto

Library of Congress Cataloging-in-Publication Data: 91-11094

1 2 3 4 5 6 7 8 9 0   DOC/DOC   9 7 6 5 4 3 2 1

ISBN   0-07-032227-9
ISBN   0-07-032228-7 {PBK}

*The sponsoring editor for this book was Joel E. Stein, the editing
supervisor was Caroline Levine, and the production supervisor was
Pamela A. Pelton. It was set in Century Schoolbook by McGraw-Hill's
Professional Book Group composition unit.*

Printed and bound by R. R. Donnelley & Sons Company.

Contents

Preface

Computer-aided design represents a quantum leap in the technology of recording an architectural project. In all previous methods of representation, from the most primitive cave markings to the most recent photoreproductive graphic systems, the recorded image was a fragmented translation of a mental model. CAD modeling redefines the graphic image as a single view of a detailed mathematical model of the project.

The 3D CAD model provides an integrated representation of the design project. It replaces the standard set of static fragmentary views. It is easily modified, and it invites change. As a workable expression of the full project, it is an instrument of both form generation and form evaluation. Given its potential for contributing to design quality and competence, CAD modeling will necessarily become a fundamental instrument of the design process.

The CAD model, in its capacity for inspection (both subjective and objective) strengthens the designer's capacity to evaluate and transform the project. As a mathematically precise statement of formal relationships, it can be directly related to performance standards and goals.

Although this graphic technology has demonstrated its economic value, several questions remain unresolved. What impact does the use of CAD have on the quality and character of the architectural product? How can CAD be best coordinated with traditional design tools and techniques? What new techniques can emerge from the design use of CAD? How should CAD skills best be acquired in the light of CAD's potential?

As technological change continues to bring CAD modeling capabilities within the reach of architects and architecture students, the CAD model will become the standard means of design communication. And although we might concern ourselves with its improving CAD teaching is a short-term issue as technology itself continues to develop a more intuitive interface. The most effective learning experience relates CAD characteristics to form generation and evaluation. In the sense that the best technology—like the best art—is self-effacing, our efforts must inevitably return to the fundamental issues of architecture itself.

The following discussion looks at CAD modeling in the context of an idealized operational model. Current graphics technology is seen as a limited subset of a more complex but integrated set of tools. As missing components become available, designers will have anticipated their introduction and will then more easily incorporate them into their working process.

This book explores one method of introducing computer-based design instruction. It seeks to place the 3D CAD model in the context of a broad integration of form generation and evaluation. By insisting on design as the framework for computer education in architecture, evolving technical possibilities can be explored while professional and artistic education is strengthened.

Acknowledgments

I am grateful for the sponsorship and encouragement of the Versacad Corporation. I appreciate the advice and encouragement of colleagues such as William K. Turner and E. Eean McNaughton. Errol Barron kindly contributed the plan of H. H. Richardson's Howard Library. Salvador Longo, Jr., contributed the model of the Tempietto. And although David Pedersen has received credit as "graphics coordinator and master plotter," that doesn't begin to speak of his contribution as an internal critic and test kitchen.

Stephen Paul Jacobs

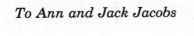

To Ann and Jack Jacobs

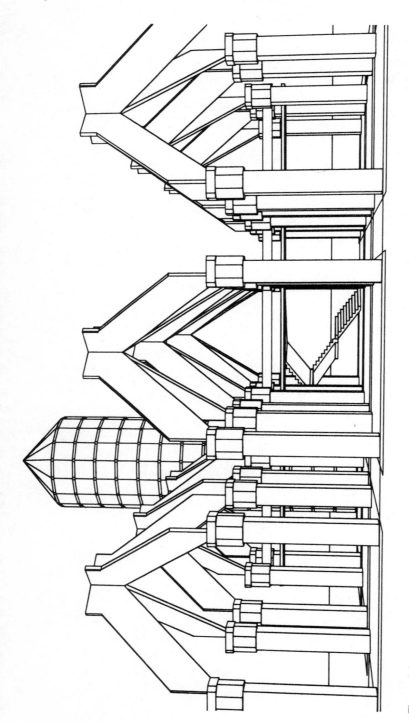

Figure 1.1

Introduction

If design is a process of understanding basic organizational and cultural themes and giving them expressive resolution, then architects require better tools to assist them in absorbing greater amounts of information and exploring more fully the consequences of alternative possibilities. Current practice involves increasingly complex programs, severe economic pressures, and broader public participation. In order that the architect play a more active role in shaping the design project, design data needs to be assimilated.

Computer modeling may indeed provide a significant means for managing this complexity. 3D CAD programs are presently both available and affordable. It is likely that these programs will continue to increase in power and ease of use but the fundamental structure of 3D CAD will remain unchanged. Experience developed with existing software will retain its value. This is an excellent time to get involved in designing with CAD.

This book may highlight the special contribution of CAD modeling to design, but a healthy process employs all available tools. The designer should not be restricted to any single graphic technique. 3D CAD modeling can be a valuable device for analyzing programmatic data, for testing alternatives, and for examining the results. Precise measurements of critical elements of the database can be analyzed and tested in terms of structure, energy, cost, and so on. These analyses can be facilitated by an increasing number of supplemental programs.

The CAD model gives the designer increased understanding and control over the elements of a project. It functions as a design intermediary by presenting a staggering amount of design information through an adjustable prism. The designer's own energy and imagination remain central to the process. CAD modeling supports the designer in identifying the inner structure of the design problem. In affording the designer the capability to pursue clearly formed ideas or intuitions at every scale of inquiry, the hope of an architecture that is alive with informed detail becomes increasingly possible.

Although CAD was initially marketed as an efficient tool for preparing working drawings, CAD modeling is a far richer and more intriguing introductory experience for the designer. In presenting an integrated three-dimensional representation of a dynamic field of design action, CAD places emphasis on the project itself rather than on separate, fragmentary views. It quickly establishes a mode of working and thinking that is entirely free of the prejudices of traditional nonelectronic graphics.

Skills developed in 3D CAD are used in CAD drafting to enhance orthographic drawings derived from the model. Since the model can generate plans, sections, and elevations, its use as the central design instrument should increase the speed and accuracy of the translation of design studies to working drawings. To fully take advantage of the possibilities of CAD, the design process and the CAD graphics process need to be well integrated.

The following discussion looks at a design process consisting of program analysis, generation of alternatives, selection, development, and evaluation. I attempt to describe the value of CAD in each of these fundamental steps. In the remaining chapters of the book I will provide exercises which will demonstrate these opportunities in the process of advancing the reader's modeling skills.

CAD and Analysis

The use of CAD modeling can be valuable at any stage of a project's development. The CAD model has both visual and mathematical characteristics. At a diagrammatic stage, its formal flexibility permits the rapid generation of a range of compositional possibilities. The database represented by each alternative represented on screen is available for a variety of comparative analyses. The model can provide a more complete representation of the project in both quantitative and qualitative terms. Computer software is available to assist in the evaluation of its quantifiable aspects. Facilities management, for example, develops an idealized three-dimensional diagram that optimizes the location of program elements in terms of functional affinities. Reports generated by such programs provide architects and clients with a common framework for discussing the needs and costs of a project. As the project and its CAD model evolve from a three-dimensional diagram to an increasingly accurate representation of the proposed building, similar analyses may be performed to provide increasingly more detailed feedback.

Visual analysis is particularly reinforced by the use of the CAD model in design. A greater variety of nonorthogonal relationships can be more easily examined. Relying on traditional orthogonal projections and laboriously constructed perspectives or axons provides too limited a set of views. The full picture of the project is constructed in the mind with minimal reinforcement. Although one's understanding of the project is still internal, the CAD model offers a more continuous and varied way to examine the model. For example, Figures I.2 to I.7 illustrate the use of the CAD model to examine shadows during different seasons and times of day. The model, of a New Orleans shotgun house, is viewed from different angles. The graphic information is

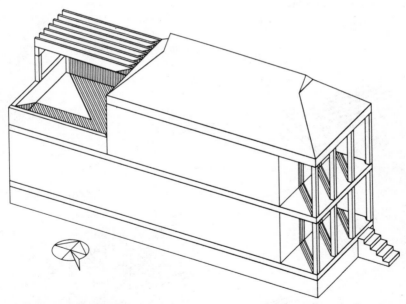

Figure I.2 Sun control analysis is facilitated by CAD modeling. The three-dimensional geometry of sun angles can accurately be compared with building geometry. Figures I.2 through I.7 present a prototypical two-story New Orleans shotgun house in parallel projection or in perspective with shadows cast according to the sun's position on the date and time indicated. Figure I.2 shows the sun's position on January 21, 9 A.M.

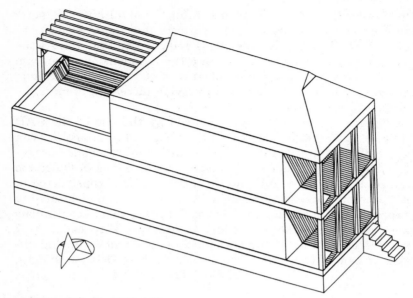

Figure I.3   July 21, 11:30 A.M.

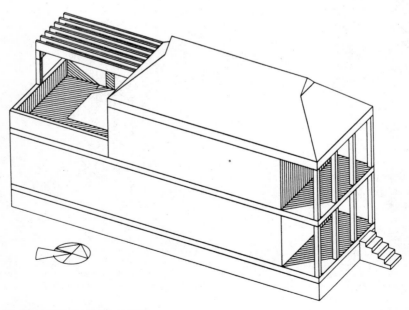

Figure I.4   January 21, 3 P.M.

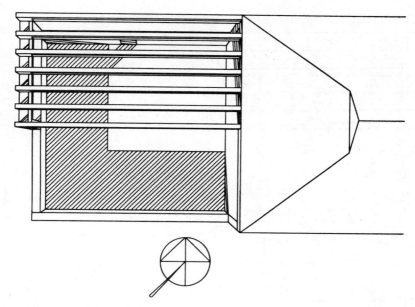

Figure I.5   January 21, 3 P.M.

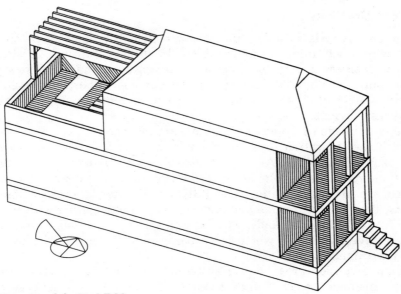

Figure I.6   July 21, 3 P.M.

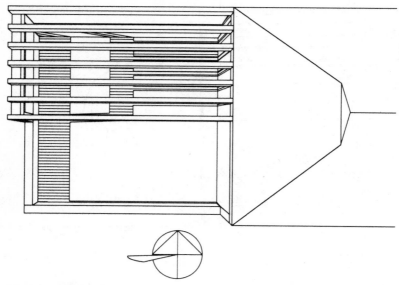

Figure I.7   July 21, 3 P.M.

more complete, and it calls for less intuitive completion. Chapter 6 develops a range of approaches to graphic analysis.

CAD and Creativity

Design creativity is an individual characteristic. It is inspired by the
challenge of each unique design problem, by the possibilities of architectural expression, and by a sense of adventure. Analytical techniques, supported by CAD, can strengthen the logical basis of design.
The role CAD can play in encouraging design invention and speculation is less obvious.

The exercises in the following chapters are intended to provide readers with the invitation to experiment with CAD capabilities. Once
space as represented in CAD is well understood, the reader is asked to
find imaginative solutions to hypothetical design projects. These
projects are often deliberately speculative to allow for less responsible
results. This playfulness may offend the designer struggling with im-
possibly conflicting demands. The intention is to emphasize a more
carefree investigation in which the software and its capabilities wel-
come experiment.

Design invention grows out of systematic and intuitive action. In
the first instance, based upon past experience, the designer generates
alternative combinations of several fundamental elements. In the sec-

ond, a more comprehensive idea is proposed and tested, and it eventually leads to new overall concepts or further systematic study. In these explorations CAD can be used effectively. In addition to recording and presenting architectural form accurately, CAD modeling facilitates a range of geometrical operations which can transform initial ideas into alternative possibilities.

The resulting dialog between the inner vision of the architect and the objective representation of that vision, as developed by the computer, enhances traditional design techniques. CAD modeling encourages a systematic approach. The very incremental nature of the CAD model calls for the reduction of more complicated forms into simpler components. These components may themselves be combined in new ways within the original form or with components of other elements suggesting unanticipated juxtapositions and relationships. The flexibility of an electronic model encourages experimentation that allows new components to be more easily placed in context, tested, and modified without the degree of commitment imposed by more traditional methods.

Although CAD models invite change and experimentation, they lack the suggestiveness and forgiving quality of loose sketches. Imprecise drawings evoke ideas that have yet to be formulated. If sweeping formal speculation is more difficult, the 3D "magic slate" welcomes speculations on its own terms. If CAD has a strong geometrical prejudice, so has the construction industry. Ideally, the designer will develop hybrid methods benefiting from impressionistic pencil graphics, rough-cut cardboard models, and CAD models organized to facilitate experimentation.

If CAD is limited to ideas which can be expressed geometrically, once those ideas are modeled, they can be expanded upon infinitely. Since the configuration of the model is independent of the position of the viewer, the presentation of new possibilities is itself flexible and provocative. Rather than fragment the project into separate views at different scales, the CAD model is actively displayed in response to the designer's curiosity. Because new views are easily available, architects can respond more completely to a developing project and inject new ideas at a greater variety of scales.

Design Development

The 3D CAD model invites a continuous development from conceptual diagram to accurate representation of a final project. Construction drawings, no longer a product of an independent graphic activity, can be seen as annotated and edited 2D views of an integrated model. Since buildings are assemblages of discrete pieces, they can be fully

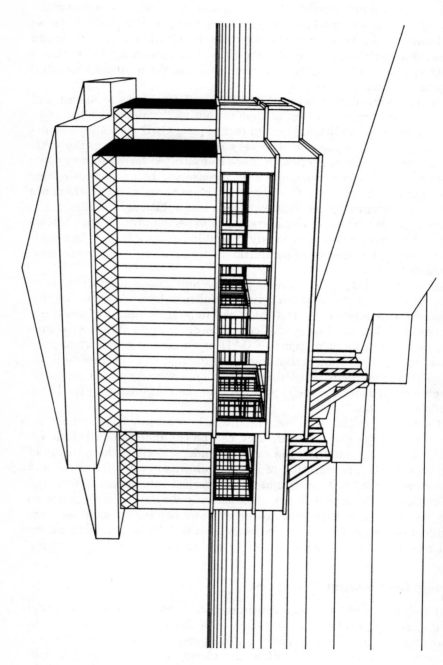

Figure 1.8 Exterior perspective from 3D model; demonstration of the kind of image generated by removing hidden lines. (*Köprülü-Yalisi, Andadoluhisari, Turkey.*)

represented by the additive structure of the CAD model. All design information is contained in a single model, which is built to real-world dimensions. Ambiguities (scale issues, discrepancies among plan, section, elevation, and projected views) inherent in 2D-based graphics are avoided.

The essential flexibility of the CAD model leads to a more resourceful process of refinement and elaboration. This ability to accommodate radical change invites freedom and responsiveness to evolving possibilities greater than those of traditional 2D pencil graphic representation. Design changes too often have unsuspected consequences. The CAD model, in displaying the project from varying points of view, make those surprises more apparent and, by providing a more complete understanding of the overall context, give the designer more opportunities to find more highly resolved solutions.

CAD Management

Working with the CAD model throughout the design process presents a series of management problems. As the CAD model becomes increasingly detailed, or as projects become larger and more complex, the CAD model becomes too dense to understand. Large projects involving several designers require standardized procedures. As the size of the database increases, basic CAD operations slow down. Fortunately, CAD programs provide opportunities to organize the model into submodels which can be displayed separately and can contain agreed-upon systems.

As a body of CAD management experience develops, convenient and standard methods of model organization will be established. Certainly, the coordination of complex projects by using traditional techniques is itself difficult. CAD has inherent management capabilities which can provide powerful support in identifying and sorting essential graphic information. The ability to select combinations of project elements for simultaneous display allows a great deal of control over the graphic information under study. The association of elements into groups or blocks permits the modification of assemblies of elements at every scale.

Taking full advantage of the digital nature of the CAD model requires prior planning. Since graphic material from other sources can easily be incorporated in the model and material generated from the current project can be useful in future work, a system of storage of an increasingly large library of model components must be developed and standardized. As the model becomes more complex, it is necessary to devise a convenient means of organizing components in useful categories that will enable the designer to extract pertinent material imme-

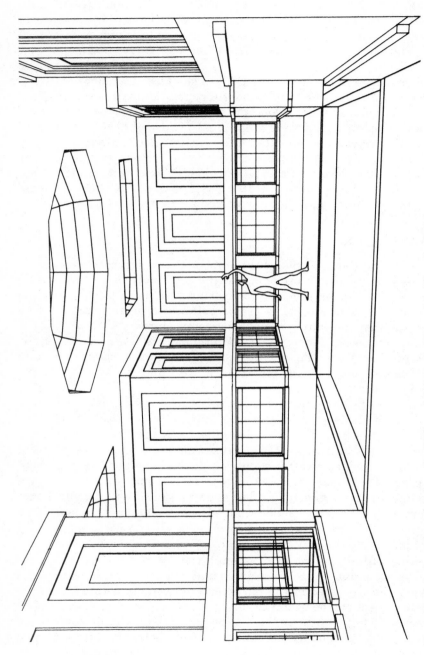

Figure I.9 Interior perspective from the CAD model shown in Figure I.8. (*Köprülü-Yalisi, Andadoluhisari, Turkey.*)

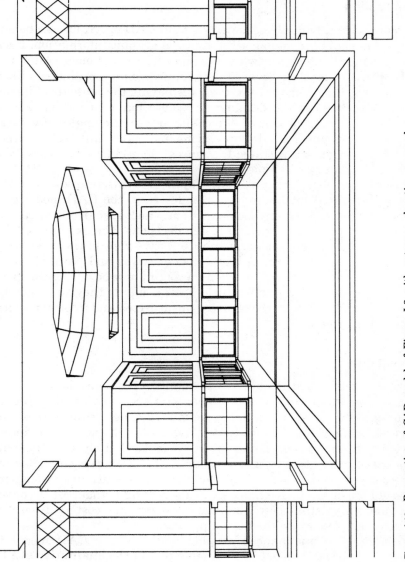

Figure I.10 Perspective of CAD model of Figure I.8 with entrance elevation removed. (*Köprülü-Yalisi, Andadoluhisari, Turkey.*)

diately while retaining the maximum flexibility for such combinations.

Visualization

Despite their individual characteristics, all CAD programs can be understood as database managers of digitized graphic information. Each has a means of entering new objects and revising old ones. (All of the CAD modeling databases record three-dimensional coordinates.) Each program has the means of selectively displaying the contents of its database. Each allows the designer to isolate material for immediate consideration from the complete model and vary the angles of view to the end of best understanding problems and opportunities. This freedom of inspection is illustrated in Figures I.11 and I.12, two views of a model of Bramante's Tempietto.

Rather than work with a limited number of discrete views of the project integrated in the mind of the designer, the CAD model provides a single working environment from which specific views can be generated in relation to specific design decisions. The experienced designer will intuitively select the most effective view of the most helpful model components. In any case, perspectives and parallel views can be generated quickly. Projected views can now be developed spontaneously. Since they require little special effort, they need not be flattering, and they may often reveal unsuspected and informative aspects of the project.

Evaluation

3D CAD models lend themselves to quantitative analysis. CAD programs allow graphic objects to be characterized as being of a specific building material with associated weight, cost, heat transmission coefficient, and so on. Software that is available can extract this information from the model's database. Mathematical analysis of the data can assist the designer to choose between alternatives at any phase of project development. New third-party software continues to support the need for quantitative analysis at each design stage. More convenient and fully detailed environmental, energy, and cost analyses can be fully integrated into the design process.

Although the unenhanced graphic image of the CAD model is highly abstract, the model is a valuable tool in the qualitative evaluation of a project. It responds to inquiry and allows for an infinite range of views. During model construction, images are selected to clarify geometric characteristics. The same visualization techniques can be applied to emphasize formal characteristics. These representa-

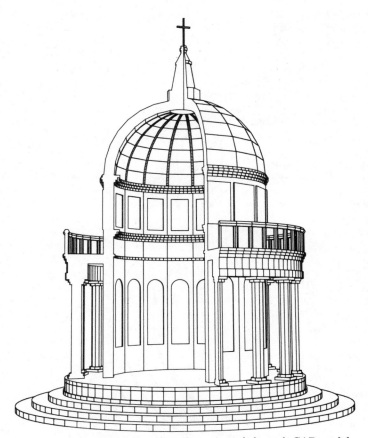

Figure I.11   Bramante's Tempietto investigated through CAD modeling, view 1. Copies of the CAD model can be freely dissected and examined without destroying the original model.

tions remain 2D projections of three-dimensional objects and, unlike physical models, cannot approach the sculptural qualities of architectural form. From another point of view, these projected drawings contain a level of detail difficult to attain in a physical model.

CAD software can include or be supplemented by rendering programs. These enhance perspective or parallel projections with accurate simulations of natural and artificial light. Color and texture may also be incorporated in the image. The realistic quality of the resulting images is dependent on specific hardware choices. At the opposite extreme, basic modeling software can generate accurate 2D images which can be edited independently of the model. These views can then be plotted and enhanced by using traditional graphic techniques. The combination of manual and computer graphics reintroduces the qual-

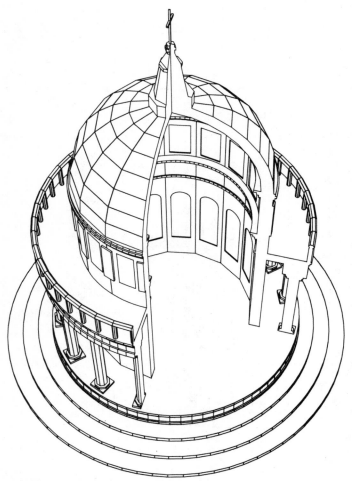

Figure I.12   Bramante's Tempietto, view 2. *Note:* Illustrations are developed from hidden-line views which are edited as two-dimensional drawings.

ity of emphasis and simplification which is inherent in pencil technique.

The CAD model has the additional advantage of being easily modified in response to criticism. Each CAD model can be reconfigured into alternative compositions. Comparisons of versions of these rapid sketch models are revealing because comparable tests can be made. Similarly, since the history of the development of the project is so easily traced, CAD offers the opportunity for a careful evaluation of the design process itself.

The final chapter of the book focuses on the use of the CAD model in qualitative analysis. The exercises take advantage of a systematic approach to model building developed in earlier chapters. These procedures are based on the ability to extract subordinate models from the project model. These resulting models are flexible and can be combined, compared, and reorganized.

Looking at CAD Critically

The adoption of CAD modeling as the central working environment for architectural design will have a major impact on both methodology and design quality. As in any change in technique, there is a corresponding change in product. In paper-based design, there is a gradual transition from suggestive imprecision to refined detail. The elements of a CAD model are always crisply defined. Their dimensions and shape may be tentative and easily modified, but their appearance speaks otherwise.

Traditional design procedures are visceral; they encourage the expression of symbol and gesture in terms of direct physical action. The connection between idea and object is much less direct in the CAD environment. On the other hand, each new element contributes to an electronic representation which invites continuing transformation. Alternative versions of ideas along with preceding experiments are available for review and adaptation, resulting in a process of great fluidity. Happily, architectural design is ecumenical and welcomes any productive approach. Hardcopy from the CAD model can form the basis for expressively tactile graphite drawings. With experience, each designer will find his or her own way to combine traditional and computer techniques.

The influence that CAD modeling has on design concepts is yet to be established. A Marshall McLuhan might see the "message of the CAD medium" as favoring incremental, geometric, repetitive, and standardized forms. CAD images as presented on the computer monitor may be so empty of qualitative content that they diminish the apparent quality of a project. On the other hand, the density and complexity of the CAD image may have its own fascination independent of the design qualities of the project itself. Frequent graphic vacations from the world of CAD model building may be necessary.

Initial explorations in CAD design can project a restrictive design process. Design work limited to any one medium constricts the designer's resourcefulness. Efforts should be made, even while emphasizing modeling experiments, to place CAD in the context of the broadest range of techniques for creating responsive and energizing architecture. An emphasis on computer-modeling techniques can not only enrich designers' CAD skills but also strengthen overall design abilities.

A Way to Learn to Model with CAD

This is a book about the design reinforcing qualities of CAD modeling rather than about the features of individual programs. I assume readers have a working knowledge of their particular CAD program including fundamental 3D operations. I assume they have available the usually excellent documentation which accompanies CAD software. I further assume that readers have completed the program tutorials and, although they have not fully mastered program commands, have a good understanding of the program's structure and the organization of reference materials.

Also, the book is directed at readers comfortable with program commands and willing to improvise new applications in response to their own design challenges. I am concerned that some readers fully experienced in CAD drafting will feel too sophisticated to play along with these exercises, yet I believe such design games are a valuable means of testing the imaginative possibilities of CAD.

Undoubtedly, as CAD modeling becomes more generally applied to design, a common body of specific computer graphics techniques will be established. My aim is to expand upon the most fundamental modeling activities, apply them to a broad range of design strategies, and encourage reader creativity both in developing architectural form and in expanding CAD possibilities.

The experience of working with 3D CAD strengthens fundamental design skills by placing them in a challenging context. In 2D design, changes tend to be first proposed in one projection and then tested in others. This is inherently a conservative process. When the model is the only active representation of the project, the impact of change can be quickly determined.

There is a joyful quality to 3D modeling which is missing from CAD drafting. Rather than work with separate fixed abstractions of a three-dimensional world, the CAD model suggests the intrigue of exploring architecture. Learning to drive the software presents immediate satisfactions unavailable in 2D CAD. An otherwise overly familiar project reveals hidden relationships.

The Impact of CAD on Architectural Education

Computer-aided design is a fact of life in architectural practice. Until recently, CAD was seen primarily as a drafting tool, and as such it

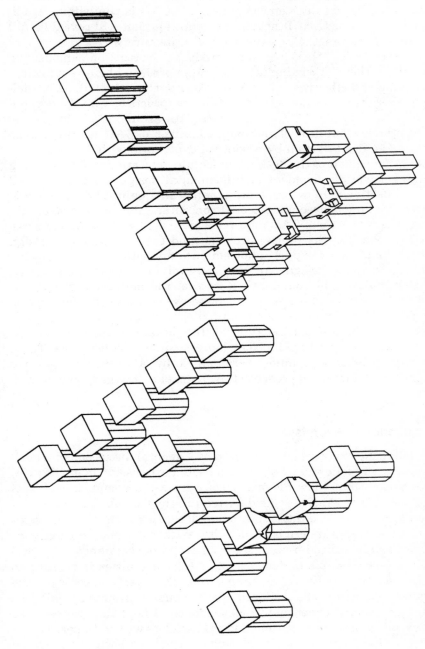

Figure I.13 Generating alternatives from a basic geometry, overview of model in which variations of columns and capitals are developed.

17

had no special appeal to design educators. With the availability of CAD modeling for desktop computers, 3D CAD is challenging traditional design practices. It needs a presentation that will reveal its full potential for strengthening the art of architecture.

The study of 3D CAD calls for a method of instruction emphasizing the integration of modeling into the design process. I believe it is more satisfying and effective to begin the study of CAD through 3D modeling rather than through computer drafting (practically and philosophically). Work in 3D CAD is immediately rewarding; it provides a fascinating representation of an imagined universe. CAD drafting can be mastered efficiently as a by-product of experience with 3D CAD.

As a component of the design curriculum, education in 3D modeling reinforces the development of fundamental design skills. The CAD model effectively allows students to integrate qualitative and quantitative thinking. Three-dimensional conceptual abilities are strengthened. The structure of CAD requires a more deliberate design process. CAD emphasizes the precise ordering and transformation of design material and raises explicit issues of form and order.

In allowing the designer to view the evolving project dynamically, CAD stimulates the imagination. At first the mechanics of monitor and mouse seem cumbersome, but hand-eye coordination develops as the CAD image becomes more familiar. Given the care that must be exercised in building a CAD model, the designer's spontaneous jottings and expression-seeking sketches take on particular value. These favorite graphic companions are joined by a dutifully attentive graphic model which approaches the dream of a drawing you can walk into.

Introduction to Exercises

The following chapters are organized as a general discussion of a modeling strategy followed by a series of design exercises. The reader will have to determine how his or her software can accomplish each specific task. The operations called for require the most fundamental program commands. The interpretation of design goals through the vehicle of a CAD program is a basic activity. With experience, the designer develops standardized procedures from program commands.

This book attempts to demonstrate CAD capabilities in relation to design strategies. Exercises range from the overly specific to the vague and fanciful. The reader is asked to puzzle through specific program actions and experiment independently. I hope this process does not cause excessive frustration and that readers will, with persistence and invention, arrive at stimulating solutions to each challenge as they develop expertise and confidence in modeling.

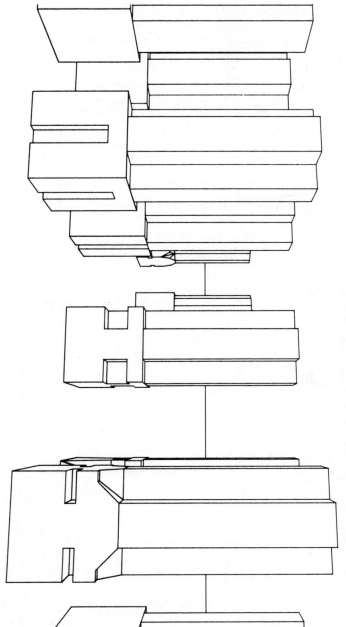

Figure I.14 Generating alternatives from a basic geometry, detailed view 1.

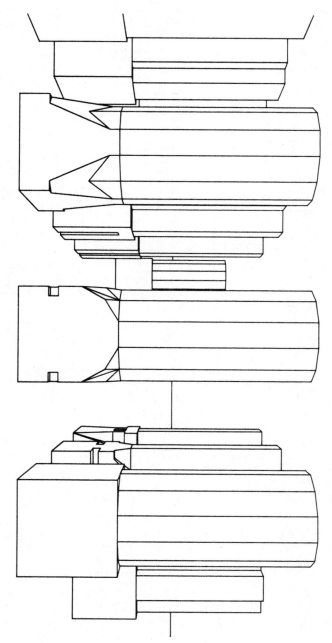

Figure I.15 Generating alternatives from a basic geometry, detailed view 2.

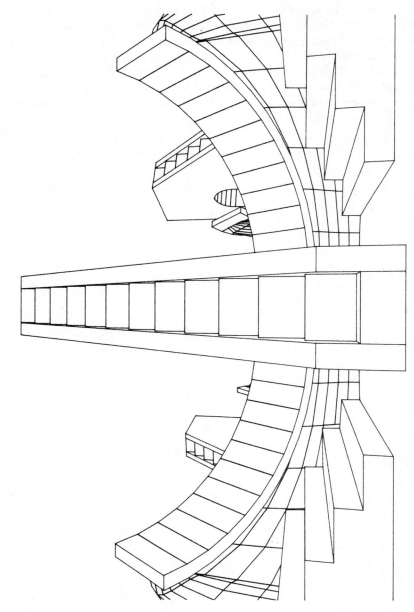

Figure 1.16 The model of an eighteenth-century stellar observatory, Jaipur, India, incorporates curved and planar surfaces.

21

The book avoids using terms specific to any particular CAD program. Since software manufacturers have often chosen the most descriptive names for their features, for the lack of better terms I have occasionally used words associated with one or another software company. I trust my readers will focus on the concepts and will translate them in terms of their own CAD programs. The reader should keep careful notes and plan the modeling process explicitly. Since designers are inventive in terms of process as well as product, it is more important to examine strategies for using CAD modeling than to examine command sequences.

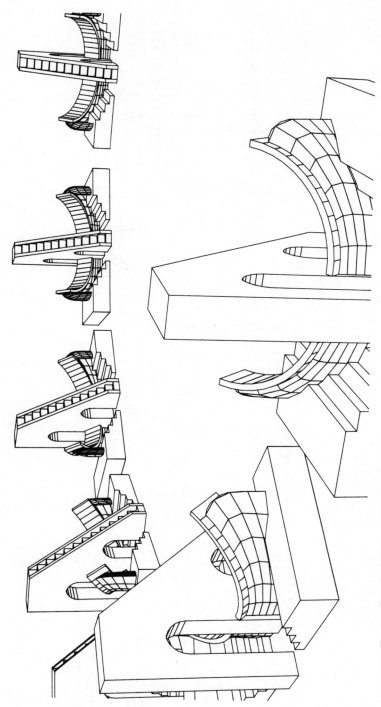

Figure 1.17 Fantasy based on Jaipur observatory.

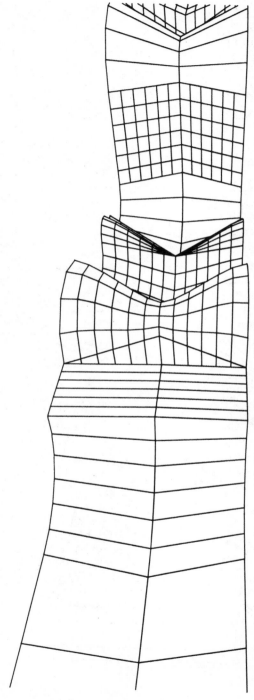

Figure 1.1 Sketch model of street space, curves derived from the profile of the base of an Ionic column.

Object Placement and Observation

Introduction

Unlike modeling with chipboard or clay, CAD model building is fundamentally an additive process. Geometric solids and surfaces supplied by the CAD program or defined by the model builder are joined to form increasingly detailed and complex objects. Initially, the complete model may be approximated strictly by the addition of simple solid volumes. This same additive process continues through every scale and stage of the model's completion.

CAD represents space on the two-dimensional surface of the computer monitor by using traditional perspective and parallel projection. Once the model is constructed, however, many additional views can be obtained by modifying the viewer's direction. These points are located in a space described by the Cartesian coordinate system. Initially, there may be some difficulty in relating the scene displayed on the screen to one's mental image of the project. With familiarity, the designer will be able to translate mental movements in relation to the project under consideration and the input of data necessary to bring about such translations on the screen.

CAD programs include shortcuts to generate parallel views and perspectives. In the beginning, it is easier to define those views by using Cartesian coordinates. As the initial basis for the construction of the model, the coordinates comprise the immediate frame of reference linking the model to real-world locations. A notebook recording the coordinates of target and viewing points is useful. Once the coordinates have been established and recorded, adjustments can be made and the resulting changes can be observed.

Cartesian coordinates place great emphasis on the origin (0,0,0).

Figure 1.2   Sketch model of street space using surfaces derived from model of Figure 1.1.

CAD programs are often geared to producing 2D plots and initially place the origin at the lower left corner of the screen. In model building, however, it is often useful to locate the origin in relation to a major point of orientation of the project itself. Later it may be necessary to change the relative position of origin and model, and that is easily accomplished.

In the early stages of a model, it is usually possible to define each new model component with points from adjacent elements. It is often convenient to assemble an object in another location and move it or copy it into place. The components remaining in this "construction yard" are available for further combination.

For designers used to conventional drafting, one of the most enjoyable discoveries when working with CAD modeling is the freedom from concerns of graphic scale. Each element of the model is given its true dimension. Detailed or comprehensive views are obtained by zooming in or out.

Naturally, the more detailed the model becomes, the greater the density of graphic material. To make the model more understandable, CAD programs allow you to sort each object into subordinate models (here referred to as subsets[1]).* Each subset, with its identifying color, can contain objects belonging to a subsystem of the building. The entire model can be read as a superimposition of these larger subordinate models. By selectively turning subsets on or off, you can focus on the aspects of the model that are of immediate concern.

*Superscript numbers are those of notes at the ends of chapters.

Construction

This exercise looks at the way three-dimensional space is represented in 3D CAD. It demonstrates the two fundamental 3D modeling skills: the accurate spatial placement space of precisely dimensioned objects and the critical observation of those objects. Repetitions of those operations will lead to a comfortable ability to form clear mental pictures of the overall model and its components reinforced by CAD projections. Based on these elementary exercises, more efficient strategies for developing the final model will be devised. As skills are improved, software mechanics will fall into place. The relationship of observer to architectural form and space will take center stage.

A simple way to initiate this process is to place two distinct objects in a clear relationship to one another. Their relative positions will be examined at a range of positions. The first object, a rectangular prism, can represent a standing human figure. The second, a cube, can represent a building module. Since the two figures are placed on a common ground plane, each view can be interpreted as a hut and a standing figure fixed in space, as seen by a moving observer.

Exercise 1.1: Object Placement

CAD modeling programs allow you to work in either perspective or parallel projection. Orthogonal views can be seen as supplementary. This emphasis on three-dimensional CAD representation will speed up a spatial understanding of the screen image. Parallel projection most clearly communicates the geometric characteristics of the model, and model construction is most easily accomplished in that view. Perspective views are more effective in conveying an experiential understanding of the model.

The first exercises provide step-by-step instructions. Often, project goals will be described and the reader will be asked to supply increasingly imaginative interpretations. Initially, an exercise's generic instructions will need translation into your CAD program's terms.

1. Open a new file, EXC1E1.

2. Select a dimensional system (feet and inches).

3. Set up a parallel projection so the model will be centered around the origin $(0,0,0)$ and viewed from the northeast. (North will be in the positive y direction)[2].

In parallel projection, the angle of view is determined by the ratios between the lengths of the x, y, z distances, and not the absolute dimensions. If we situate ourselves at a point $50', -50', 50'$, we will be

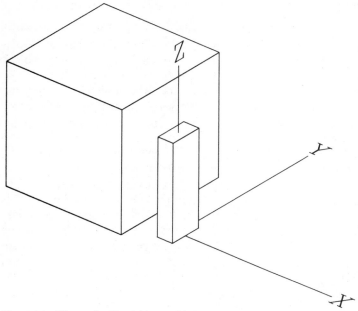

Figure 1.3 Figure for Exercise 1.2, basic Cartesian orientation.

looking down at the model and toward the northwest. Three lines along the x, y, and z axes will temporarily provide orientation as illustrated in Figure 1.3.

4. Draw a line from the origin (0,0,0) to 10′,0,0 (a 10′ line along the positive x-axis), a line from 0,0,0 to 0,10′,0 (a 10′ line along the positive y-axis), and a line from 0,0,0 to 0,0,10′ (a 10′ vertical line).

5. Begin the model by placing a rectangular prism representing a human figure directly above the origin on the ground plane ($z = 0$). The figure should measure 6′ high by 2′ wide and 1′ deep and should face due east, along the x-axis. (In a future exercise you will be asked to model a more realistic scale figure.)

6. Place a 7′6″ cube on the ground plane to the west of our figure. Its faces should also be parallel to the x, y, and z axes. Locate one corner at point $-2′$, $-2′$,0. The opposite diagonal corner should be placed at $-9′6″$,5′6″,7′6″.

This cube, once copied and added to itself (in the manner of a block set), could produce understandable architectural volumes. For the moment, however, let us use our mannequin and block to explore viewing a CAD model.

Save the model as file 1EX1.

Observation

CAD model building is a conversation between the developing mental picture of the project and the evolving representation. Initially, this mental image will indicate views for model construction and evaluation. Once projected, adjustments will be made to further define the model's geometry and simplify construction.

With experience, the translation of anticipated mental pictures into software commands becomes intuitive. Eventually, you will be able to move through the project mentally with the immediate and accurate support of the CAD model. Both the physical (chipboard, clay, and so on) and the CAD model emphasize geometry, but the CAD model, through perspective drawings, conveys experiential qualities. The CAD model is flexible and invites change. The laboriously glued physical model resists such experimentation.

Throughout the design process, the CAD model can be used to generate perspective and parallel views in response to design questions. View parameters can be saved so that alternative schemes can be evaluated from the same vantage point. The careful alternation between design, model construction, and evaluation suggests a thought process that is both rigorous and exploratory.[4]

CAD programs on the microcomputer ordinarily present solid objects as wire frame constructions, which display all of the edges of component planes. Surfaces are fully transparent. For a more realistic view of an opaque model, the software will remove hidden lines. In this often time-consuming process, the position of each edge of each object is mathematically compared to every other edge of every object in viewer's range of vision. The more complex the model, the slower the process.[3] While hidden-line drawings are often valuable, with experience the wire frame model is quite sufficient. Color can be used to identify families of objects and thereby further clarify the model. Rendering programs can enhance projected views by applying color and texture to the visible surfaces while shading the planes in relation to a given light source.

The value of the interaction between the designer and the computer depends on an ability to translate mental images into CAD terms and to construct an accurate mental image from the graphic material presented by the computer. The exercises that follow are intended to focus on that dialog.

Exercise 1.2: Viewing Objects

For the first exercise in observing a CAD model, circle around the two objects from Exercise 1.1.

1. Starting from a point due east of the cube and, moving in a counterclockwise direction, construct a series of perspectives at 45° intervals.

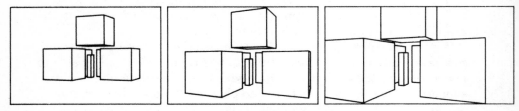

Figure 1.4   Figure for Exercise 1.3, sequence of views approaching inner space.

2. Establish the center of interest (target) above the origin at a height of 5'6" (0,0,5'6").

3. Begin the tour at a distance 50' to the east of the objects. Maintain an eye level of 5'6" to simulate a standing observer. The coordinates of the first observation point will be 50'0",0, 5'6".

Adjust the distance between the objects and the viewer to fill the screen with the model. Your software probably has several ways to accomplish that. Initially, enter each location by its coordinates. Make any adjustments until you are satisfied with the view. Note the coordinates of each new observation point for reference later in the exercise. As the model develops, identical views of the model will be compared.

4. Circle the two volumes a second time but from a higher vantage point (a second story). Add 10' to the viewing height. Make note of these locations.

5. Compare related views from ground level and from the second level.

6. Repeat the process by using parallel projection. Place the observer on the same ground plane as the model and view the model from due east.

7. Circle in a clockwise direction in 45° increments. Zoom in to fill the screen with the model's image.

8. Repeat the experiment from a higher vantage point, let's say 50'. Compare perspectives and parallel views seen from the same direction.

When working in 3D CAD, it is important to understand that elevation and plan are special cases of parallel projection which occur when the viewpoint is along a primary axis.

9. Select the most characteristic perspective and isometric and plot each wire frame view.

10. Plot hidden-line views of each projection.

As already mentioned, as models become more complex, hidden-line drawings become increasingly time-consuming. Rather than invest

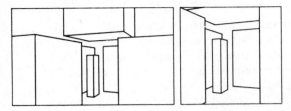

Figure 1.4 *(Continued*

computer time in ephemeral screen images, save the hidden-line views to 2D files. These drawings can be edited by working within CAD and, once plotted, as the basis of traditional computer-free graphic explorations.

Save hidden-line views as 1EX2A, 1EX2B, etc.

Exercise 1.3: Adding Objects to Form a Space

In this exercise, new objects will be added to the preceding scene to suggest a more complex environment.

1. Copy file 1EX1 as 1EX3 and then load the new file.

2. Working in parallel projection, arrange three copies of the original 7'6" cube to form a space surrounding the scale figure.

All objects should rest on the ground plane. The cubes should be separated by at least 30" to allow views into the space. These gaps will become particularly useful when the transparent wire frame views are replaced by hidden-line drawings.

3. Pile additional cubes on the first four to develop a more compete enclosure.

4. Working in perspective, explore the new complex as a whole; repeat the clockwise tour recommended in Exercise 1.2. Note the coordinates of particularly revealing views.

5. At eye level, prepare a series of five hidden-line perspectives representing a sequence of views approaching the inner space on foot.

Figure 1.4 presents one such sequence. Save these views as slides or plots. How deep can you get into the space before the image loses coherence? If the walls of the space were further subdivided, would the image be easily read at closer range?

6. Replace one of the cubes forming the space with a thin rectangular prism representing a wall one foot thick.

7. Reconstruct key perspectives and observe any resulting changes.

8. Substitute walls for each of the cubes while retaining the dimensions of the interior space. Review the preceding views.

9. It is often useful to place temporary objects in the model; they help define the location of more-permanent model components. As an example, insert the largest possible prism within the interior space just developed. Move it horizontally along the x or y axis so that it is adjacent to the original space.

10. Using this new volume as a spatial jig, copy and place wall elements to form enclosing planes. In Figure 1.5, dashed lines are used to represent the temporary cubes. Make sure to allow for circulation between spaces.

11. Once the space is defined, move the jig to a third location and continue adding wall elements. Finally, delete the jig.

Spend time exploring this graphic world while testing the ability of your software to convey spatial information. Place copies of the original scale figure in several locations within the complex to reinforce a sense of relative dimension.

Save the model as file 1EX3.

These short exercises demonstrate a simple additive process for developing complex spaces and solid objects. Most model-building procedures are elaborations of these incremental strategies. Later chapters will discuss procedures allowing you to work with compound compo-

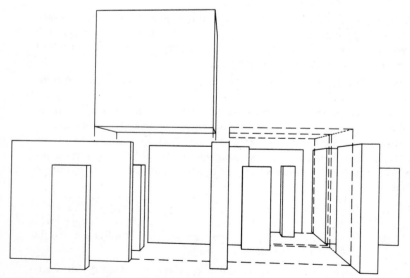

Figure 1.5   Figure for Exercise 1.4, demonstrating the use of spatial jigs.

nents. Yet even those procedures are fundamentally additive and sub-tractive.

Notes

1. *Notes on terminology:* In attempting to write a book focusing on design rather than on software, I have frequently been faced with problems of terminology. CAD system developers have appropriated common English words to describe specific aspects of their programs. Frequently they have chosen different words for essentially the same feature. At the same time, there are a limited set of concise and yet descriptive words. I hope my choice of terms will clarify rather than confuse fundamental concepts.

   The two features which allow the designer to manage collections of objects are *groups* and *subsets*. I have used these terms throughout the book as most descriptive. The more usual *level* and *layer* are rooted in the use of transparent tracing paper and the primary organization of buildings into horizontal strata. I prefer "subset" in that it is spatially neutral. It refers to the selection of aspects of the model for display.

   On the other hand, the terms *blocks* and *groups* present a more difficult problem. I see collective objects used in a variety of ways: in some instances, as permanent and recurring combinations of objects; in others, as temporary but convenient assemblages useful for one operation or transformation and never to be used again. I prefer the flexible invitation to experiment with a *group* rather than the more solid, permanent-sounding, *block*.

2. Throughout this book, spatial locations will be referred to by their coordinates in an x, y, z order. For example, a point located at $x = 50', y = 50', z = 50'$ will be referred to as at $50', 50', 50'$.

3. Faster computers make their greatest contribution to model building here.

4. *Notes on setting up a perspective:* As an architect, working in real-world terms, the most comfortable introductory technique for setting up a perspective is to use x, y, and z coordinates to specify target (center) and station point (camera point). Make notes of these initial coordinates and make final adjustments by comparing numbers to images. Once you are familiar with a digital approach, software features dependent on using graphic means can be relied upon.

Editing Objects

Introduction

In Chapter 1, you built CAD models one object at a time; in this chapter you will begin to explore larger-scale operations. Basic editing commands, essential to 2D drafting, have creative implications when applied to model building.

CAD modeling programs allow you to copy objects at equal intervals to form linear, planar, or volumetric *arrays*. In the early stages of a model, it is often useful to introduce a three-dimensional array of cubes to provide a visual reference and to more easily place model elements. These cubes should be assigned to their own graphic subset with a distinct color. During the course of the project, additional elements may be required to provide specific dimensional assistance. CAD programs provide *snap modes* which restrict cursor placement to multiples of a given dimension. This feature, along with the temporary use of reference solids, can increase your speed and provide greater accuracy in determining positions in 3D space. When the model is more developed and there are enough spatial reference points, this temporary prop is no longer needed and can be turned off or erased.

The sequence of exercises in this chapter will develop the idea of using basic editing commands effectively and imaginatively. The first exercise uses previously developed material to build an heroic space. Perspective views will allow the space to be examined inside and out. The abstract elements originally used to define the space will be replaced with more representational components. This procedure will suggest an interactive method of working at multiple scales. In later exercises, we will examine the model critically to suggest alternative space-defining solutions.

Exercise 2.1: Supercube (Copy and Remove)

In Exercise 1.1, a scale figure was placed next to a rectangular volume of fixed dimensions; in this exercise, a large space will be carved out of a giant cube. Once the space is defined, a cubic person and a sphere will be placed in the space to provide contrasting elements for further study.

1. Place a 7'6" cube so that one corner sits on the origin (0,0,0) and the diagonal opposite corner is placed at −7'6", −7'6",7'6".

2. Use the array and copy commands to produce a 5 × 5 × 5 supercube consisting of 125 copies of the 7'6" cube. Leave a 2'6" gap between adjacent cubes. This gap will allow you to view inside hidden-line drawings.

3. Remove the 27 interior cubes so that only the surface cubes remain. The resulting model should develop an interior space measuring 32'6" along each axis.

4. Place a 18'-diameter sphere asymmetrically within the 32'6" cube. The sphere should be centered at coordinates 20',20',10'.

In 3D CAD, curved surfaces are approximated by three- or four-sided planes. The greater the number of sides, the closer the approximation but the larger the database (resulting in longer times for regeneration and hidden-line removal). For convenience, the sphere can be approximated roughly. (CAD programs differ in the manner of controlling the smoothness of curved surfaces).

5. Add a mannequin (6' tall, 2' wide, and 1' deep) oriented north-south at coordinates 12',12',0. The model is illustrated in Figure 2.1.

Exercise 2.2: Observation

1. While using the mannequin and the sphere for reference, generate a sequence of perspectives approaching the entire model along a single axis. Note the coordinates of each view.

2. Center the view behind the cubic mannequin at coordinates 12',12',5'6".

3. Place the observer at coordinates 250',12',5'6". (Adjust the distance along the x-axis so the overall model fills the screen.) Resulting views should place the scale figure consistently at the center of the monitor.

4. Move in closer; reduce the distance between the observer and the mannequin successively by half. When the projection of the model no longer makes sense, pull away from the figure and di-

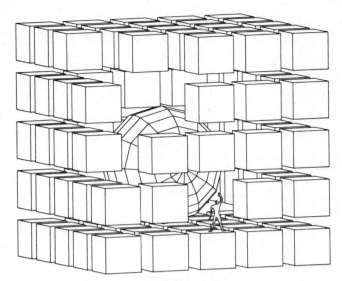

Figure 2.1   Figure for Exercise 2.1, supercube.

rect your view up into the interior of the space by choosing a new, higher, target.

5. Select the most characteristic views in the series and save them as hidden-line slides or plots.

6. Experiment with other pairs of viewpoints and targets. Take advantage of the unique elements to help orient you within the supercube.

7. Save the model as file 2EX2 and again as 2EX2A.

8. Load the file 2EX2A.

9. Remove several of the 7'6" cubes from the exterior shell of the supercube to open up a better view of the interior.

10. Develop a revealing perspective view of the model and experiment enhancing the image with the software's shade utility.

11. Experiment with variations on light direction and intensity. Keep careful notes to assist you in developing an effective method for future use.

Exercise 2.3: Creative Removal

The structure of CAD modeling programs implies an additive process. It is also possible to work subtractively by deleting or "carving out" material. This exercise demonstrates the approach.

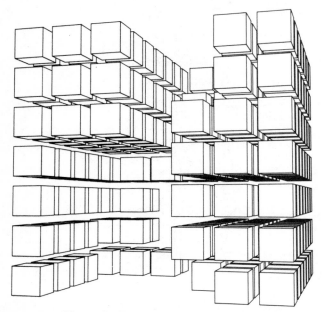

Figure 2.2   Figure for Exercise 2.2, example of form resulting from initial excavations.

1. As in Exercise 2.2, place a 7′6″ cube with one corner at the origin (0,0,0) and the opposite diagonal corner at − 7′6″, − 7′6″,7′6″.

2. Use the array and copy commands to build a 7 × 7 × 7 cube with 2′6″ separations between component cubes. For clarification, place each horizontal plane of cubes in a different subset. Each subset should have its own color.[1]

3. Save the model as file 2EX3.

4. Consider the 67′6″ cube a piece of abstract clay. Delete enough blocks to produce two intersecting spaces of different shapes and dimensions. Make one space fully contained within the 7 × 7 × 7 cube; the other should reach the exterior (Figure 2.2).

To delete interior cubes, it may be necessary to turn off upper subsets of the model.

5. Once you are satisfied with your spatial composition, save the model as file 2EX3A.

Notes on hidden-line images

With current microcomputers, CAD software displays models as wire frame images. Initially, this may feel uncomfortably abstract, and the modeler will repeatedly call for hidden-line views for a more realistic representation. With experience, wire frame models will be less objectionable; in fact, the model's transparency will be a great advantage. Hidden-line constructions will be performed mentally, and the screen image will be understood less literally. CAD hidden-line plots could approach the spare suggestiveness of Paul Letarouilly's drawings of Rome if one could master his subtle use of line weight (Figure 2.3).

At the time of writing, most microcomputer CAD programs were using wire frame modeling and surfaces were defined in the CAD database by their edges. Surface- and solid-modeling software that is available for more powerful computers is able to consider surfaces and solids directly. In a wire frame environment, the projection of a hidden-line image of the model requires computation. Each edge in the database is compared with other edges to determine if it is eclipsed when viewed from the current angle. As the model grows, the number of these comparisons increases exponentially.

In order to speed up the process, you must reduce the number of edges being evaluated. Turn off all subsets that will not be seen in the desired view. Always develop a 2D CAD file of the hidden-line image. This drawing file can be used for minor modifications and for experimentation without requiring the construction of new hidden-line drawings.

Evaluation and choice

3D CAD modeling facilitates the development of alternative interpretations of a single idea. Elements can readily be modified and reorganized. Variations can be saved for future reference. A design technique based on theme and variations lends itself to critical evaluation and the generation of alternative solutions. The following exercises demonstrate this flexibility.

3D CAD supports an articulate design process; it makes use of both quantitative and qualitative techniques for comparing alternatives. The model database contains valuable information, once a body of available techniques is developed for its extraction. The flexibility of the display of graphic information along with the editing power of the software allows a clear and swift transition from analysis and the generation and testing of alternatives.

This book emphasizes qualitative analysis; since the CAD model has a mathematical basis, it can be tested quantitatively (heat loss, solar gain, adjacency, cost, density). The model can be evaluated at any stage of the design process and, along with visual procedures, side-by-side comparisons of current alternatives along with preceding solutions are facilitated.

Figure 2.3 *Vue de Vestibule et de l'Escalier, Palais Corsini, Via della Longara* from Paul Letarouilly, *Edifices de Rome Moderne,* Paris, 1860 (reprinted by *Princeton Architectural Press,* 1982).

Exercise 2.4: Variations on a Theme

This exercise will further develop the form you carved out from the 7 × 7 × 7 cube. By generating several alternative compositions from the same material, you will illustrate the flexibility of CAD modeling in transforming basic material. This set of solutions will give you the opportunity to apply identical criteria to each variation. Since the models represent formal ideas, these evaluations will have an aesthetic basis. In building design, the component volumes will be built of different materials and will enclose different uses. Using subsets and groups to identify materials and function will permit a more complex analysis.

The composition developed in file 2EX3A will be the basis of the following experiments. The "supercube" of 7′6″ cubes can be organized into rows and columns.

1. Replace each row or column of cubes with a rectangular prism.
2. Develop three alternative schemes for this recomposition. For example, the interior spaces could be defined only by horizontal prisms parallel to the x-axis. Another extreme solution would use vertical prisms. A third would combine horizontal and vertical elements.
3. The three solutions should be saved as files 2EX4A, 2EX4B, 2EX4C. Figure 2.4a to c presents one interpretation.
4. Establish three perspective views which clarify the relation between the two carved spaces and the large cube.
5. By using these vantage points, save three hidden-line perspectives of each of the three schemes (2EX4C1, 2EX4C2, etc.). Each of the three alternatives can be seen as a distinct approach to a design issue.
6. Use plots of all nine drawings to help you compare the characteristics of each scheme.
7. Based upon your observations, generate a fourth solution which more richly defines the inner spaces and the outer envelope while restricting defining elements to prisms parallel to the x, y, and z axes.

The excavated supercube can be seen as containing three orders of space: the two excavated spaces, the 2′6″ shafts of space between cubes, and the spaces within the cubes themselves. Devise your own experiments to work with the interplay among these three spatial modules. For example, pairs of planes 7′6″ × 7′6″ × 6″ placed 6′6″ apart can substitute for the original cubes. Pairs can be oriented horizontally or vertically. Individual square surfaces can be joined

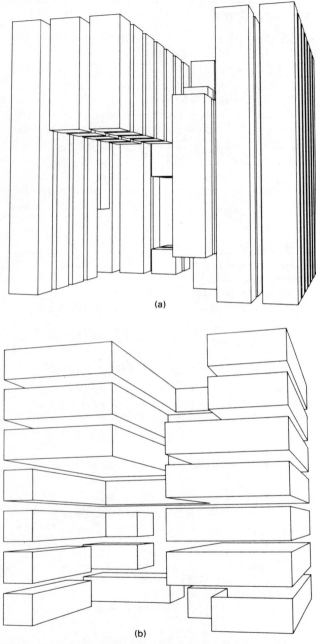

(a)

(b)

Figure 2.4   Exercise 2.4: (a) vertical, (b), horizontal, and (c) combined vertical and horizontal prisms substituted for cubes in Figure 2.2.

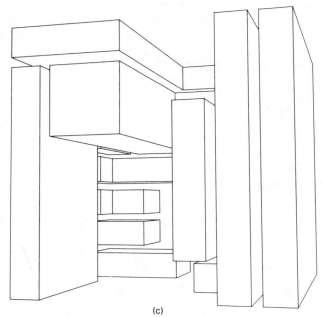

(c)

Figure 2.4 (*Continued*) Exercise 2.4: (*a*) vertical, (*b*), horizontal, and (*c*) combined vertical and horizontal prisms substituted for cubes in Figure 2.2.

to form more continuous bands. Explore the resulting model by using previously developed vantage points. Insert scale figures where useful. Reconstruct the perspective views used in the preceding studies and save the most interesting views as hidden-line drawings.

Repetitive copy

For practical and aesthetic reasons, buildings are composed of repetitive elements at one scale or another. Prototype models of these elements can be developed from simple geometric solids. They can be further refined by the addition of surfaces stretched between spatial points determined by the solids. Standard or custom elements from 3D CAD libraries can be introduced into the model. These quotations can supply temporary details and a sense of scale. Together, they can be copied to specific locations, or they may form an array sketching larger-scale building organizations. This approach reflects J.-N.-L. Durand's theoretical exercises of 1821 illustrated in Figure 2.5.

Previously, the copy command was used to establish a dimensional

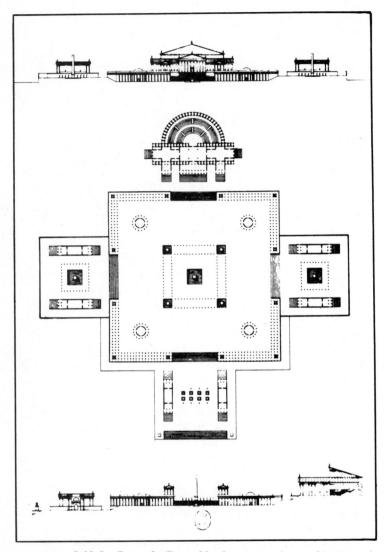

Figure 2.5 J.-N.-L. Durand, *Ensemble formé par la combinaison de plusieurs edifices*, from the *Partie Graphique*, 1821 (*reprinted in Robin Middleton (ed.),* The Beaux-Arts and Nineteenth-Century French Architecture, *MIT Press, 1982*).

framework for the model. In the following exercises, the copy command will be used to introduce newly modeled subcomponents to locations within the model. A single flight of stairs will be modeled and added to a library of basic planning elements. This component will be a basic part of the remaining models in this chapter.

The stair is a useful example of repetitive form. As a three-dimensional diagonal, it tests spatial perception. As a fundamental component of a building's movement system, its dynamic sculptural and spatial qualities give it an important role in architectural expression. As the stair is refined from its schematic basis through detailed elaboration, the evolution of a CAD model from planning tool to representation can be understood. Chapter 4 will discuss the development of such a fully detailed stair along with a system for exchanging representational and schematic elements.

Exercise 2.5: Repetitive Copy, Modeling a Stair

This exercise will be conducted in two stages. Initially, develop a schematic model of a straight run and save it as a group. Later, you will copy the group and combine it with landings to form more elaborate stairs. For simplicity, the schematic stair should consist only of treads. After planning and constructing the staircase, the schematic elements will be replaced with more developed components.

For this exercise, the floor-to-floor distance is 15'0". For flexibility, the vertical run will be divided in thirds, resulting in a unit which can be combined with landings to produce a variety of stairs. The unit run measures 3'8" wide, with a 10" tread and a 7½" riser (omitted in the schematic model). The tread at landing level should be included. The unit run should be saved as a group with the name STAIR1. A 3'8" × 3'8" square should be defined and saved as the group LAND1. Initially, the landing contains only one object; defining it as a group facilitates later substitutions.

Use STAIR1 and LAND1 to build models of standard straight-run, scissors, and U-type stairs. Once you are familiar with inserting groups into the current model, copying them, and placing them in space, experiment with the following models:

1. A lighthouse with its lantern 60' above the cliff requires an exterior stair to the top. The stair wraps around the 20'-square structure supporting the lantern. Save this model as 2EX5A.

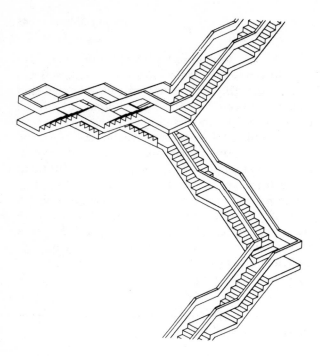

Figure 2.6 Exercise 2.5, parallel projection of square stair.

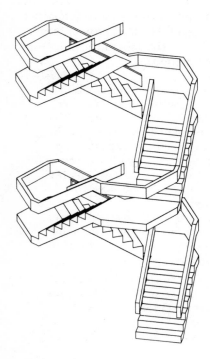

Figure 2.7 Exercise 2.5, parallel projection of triangular stair.

2. An alternative solution calls for a free-standing stair forming a triangular spiral. The stair connects to the 20' × 20' square tower only at the top. Model this stair and test alternative positions in relation to the tower. In this instance, you will need to add a diamond-shaped landing (two adjacent 3'8" equilateral triangles) to your kit of parts (LAND1A). Save this model as 2EX5B.

3. Develop interesting parallel and perspective views of these models. Note the coordinates so that the same views can be reconstructed. Save hidden-line drawings of the most interesting views.

4. Once the series of schematic designs has been completed, return to the construction yard and proceed to refine the unit stair and the two landings. Give thickness to treads and landings. Add risers. Provide structure, handrails, and balusters. Save the elaborated unit run as the group STAIR2. Likewise, form groups of both landings (LAND2, LAND2A). Finally, replace the groups used to plan the preceding stairs with elaborated components.

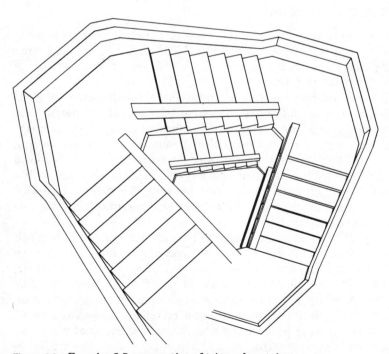

Figure 2.8   Exercise 2.5, perspective of triangular stair.

Exercise 2.6: Erector Set

Work with schematic components to develop a new model incorporating the triangular and square spiral stairs from the preceding exercises. Use group commands to arrange copies of rectangular and triangular stair towers on the ground plane. Develop standard bridges to connect selected landings on one stair tower to landings at the same elevation on adjacent towers.

View the resulting composition in perspective from ground level. Walk around this Piranesian construct and select particularly expressive views for hidden-line construction and plotting. View the model from one of the bridges 30′ above the ground and develop perspective views looking toward a nearby stair tower with distant towers beyond.

Develop a second perspective by standing at the top of a flight of stairs and looking into the deep space of the stairwell. Once you are satisfied with each view, substitute the more-developed versions of the model's components. Save key views as slides and plots. Save the model as 2EX6.

Exercise 2.7: The Labyrinth

Armed with the ability to copy in three dimensions, generate non-orthogonal elements, and make use of a CAD library, it is about time that we construct an electric labyrinth rich in symbolism and full of adventure, fantasy, and mystery.

3D CAD gives us opportunities unimagined by the designers of British hedge mazes, who felt constrained to extrude 2D patterns into space. Movement over and under gives us powerful new opportunities to baffle and surprise. The tantalizing geometric overview, giving false reassurance of an easy order, is replaced by the confusion and fear of the depths of the labyrinthine experience. Mazes come to life through participation, not abstract admiration. The refusal of minor elements to adhere to rigid symmetry creates a world of general uniformity but specific confusion.

In the context of mastering 3D modeling, the design of a labyrinth has several educational objectives. It presents a design challenge which tests basic model-building procedures. A few components (stair, bridge, and wall) can be used to create a world of imagination. The game of transforming order into confusion challenges the imagination and yet provides an inherent discipline for criticism. The exaggerated interdependence of high panoramas and channeled internal views reinforces the need for alternating views frequently during the modeling process.

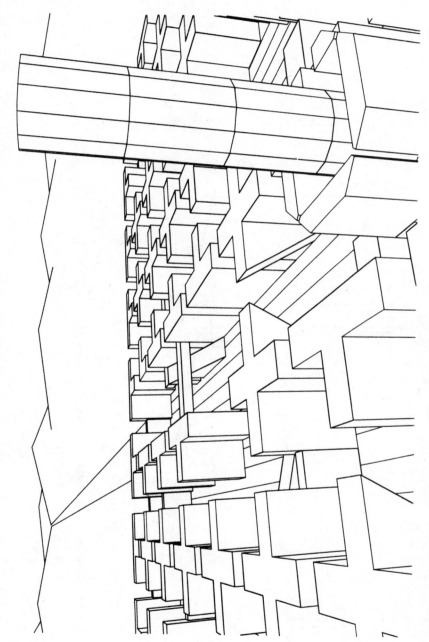

Figure 2.9 Exercise 2.7, view from tower of a labyrinth based on repetitive cruciform elements.

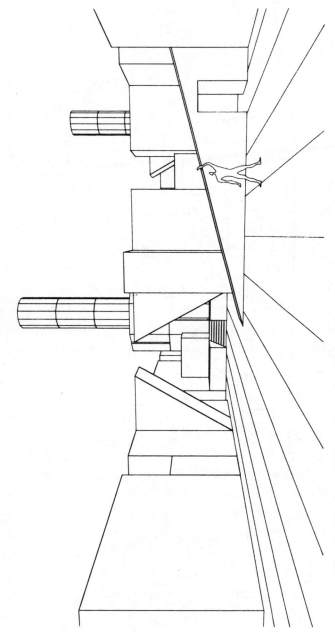

Figure 2.10 Exercise 2.7, view within the labyrinth of Figure 2.9.

1. Use the stair elements developed in the preceding exercise. Add unit walls to form corridors and to support unit bridges. These three elements should, when copied and positioned, produce an intriguing and bewildering place.

2. Develop one principal space, the location of the treasure, the goal of the labyrinthine tour. Make it difficult to get to but easy to escape from.

3. Along the path, provide overlooks with broad perspectives of the entire construction giving false reassurance of victory and leading immediately into the areas of greatest confusion.

Notes

1. *Warning:* Like a sorcerer's apprentice, the array command is capable of developing huge files, particularly when objects are copied in three dimensions. Depending on the computer's speed, the 343 cubes just created will significantly slow down regenerations and hidden-line removals.

3

Custom Objects

Introduction

As models evolve from general massing studies to detailed represen-
tations, custom-made components must be added to program-supplied
geometric volumes. The partnership between CAD modeling and traditional graphics is well established. Less well defined is a working
relationship between the traditional physical model and the CAD
model. Because of the mathematical nature of CAD, there is a built-in
geometric bias. If CAD modeling can fully become the medium for architectural design, it must be able to conveniently translate sculptural vision into CAD modeling terms. This chapter will look at such
procedures.

As models evolve from abstraction to representation, the number of
surfaces in the model increases, especially with the introduction of
curves. The organized use of subsets and other strategies which allow
for the temporary substitution of simpler elements for more fully modeled components was introduced in Chapter 2. The focus of this chapter is on the fully realized model and the value of the model in design
evaluation and the generation of construction drawings.

The purpose of the following exercises is to explore methods of working with program-generated volumes along with custom-made objects
to develop a full range of architectural forms. In general, built-in volumes can be used to sketch volumetric characteristics. They can also
provide necessary points in space. The use of subsets with assigned
colors can distinguish these temporary spatial jigs from the newly
modeled objects. Once all construction aids have been removed, the
fully developed component can be saved for future use and imported
into the principal model.

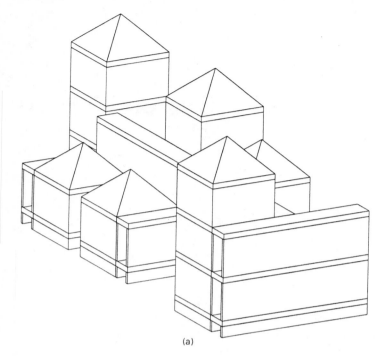

(a)

Figure 3.1   Massing Experiments.

Exercise 3.1: Roof Geometries

Roofs are common building elements which often require special modeling attention. Formal issues, plan geometry, sun control, and drainage often result in complex three-dimensional intersections as exemplified by the model illustrated in Figure 3.2 on page 57. CAD modeling can establish precise dimensional characteristics comfortably while inviting modification and refinement.

1. Use the outline of a house plan with two or more perpendicular wings to model a hip roof with a 5-in-12 slope.

2. The insertion of temporary elements will be useful to establish precise spatial locations. On a subset reserved for these spatial jigs, place pyramids with 5-in-12 slopes at the ends of each wing with bases equal to the wing's width.

3. Copy the pyramids to the intersection of the wings to establish the points where each lower ridge intersects the plane of the higher roof. The final roof surface will use some of the faces of the pyramids along with new roof planes formed by connecting ridges and eaves.

4. Repeat the exercise with wings intersecting at angles other than

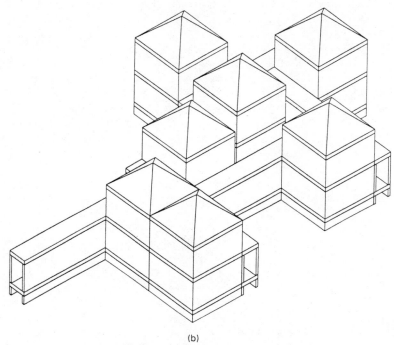

(b)

Figure 3.1   (*Continued*) Massing Experiments

90°. In these instances, the pyramids with 5-in-12 slopes can still be used to establish ridge locations.

5. Enrich the sculptural qualities of the roof by introducing dormers, domes, and turrets. You may need to improvise other dimensional jigs by using the vocabulary of simple solid objects provided by the software.

Exercise 3.2: The Sculptural Connection

Konrad Wachsmann would have loved CAD modeling. In his 1961 book, the *Turning Point of Building,* he illustrates the importance of connections in the industrialization of buildings. The spatial implications of the geometries suggested by his structures are brilliantly presented. Figure 3.3*a* to *c* presents a reconstruction as a CAD model of one of Wachsmann's proposals. For our purposes, the design of small-scale structural connections provides an opportunity to strengthen modeling skills and link them to formal invention.

As Wachsmann demonstrated, the design of the joint is key to the development of the space frame. This exercise presupposes a space

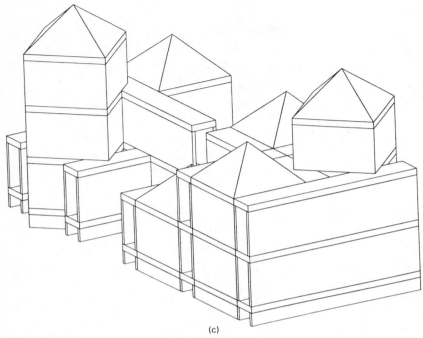

(c)

Figure 3.1   (*Continued*) Massing Experiments

frame design (a three-dimensional truss similar in geometry to the Unistrut system). Develop a molded joint, to be used throughout the truss, capable of connecting eight members. Two square 5'0" grids are placed horizontally to form the upper and lower chords of the truss. The two horizontal grids are shifted one-half module in the x and y directions. They are separated by members placed at three-dimensional diagonals. These diagonals form upright pyramids with their apexes at the upper intersections and inverted pyramids converging at the lower grid's intersections.

Assuming the horizontal and diagonal members are steel pipes with a 2" diameter, design a component which would handsomely connect the four horizontal and four diagonal tubes. Consider ways to attach the pipe to the joint. The pipes may be given special fittings at their ends; nonetheless you should seek a solution with the fewest elements. This exercise may be one instance in which a physical sketch model may be particularly useful in developing the CAD model.

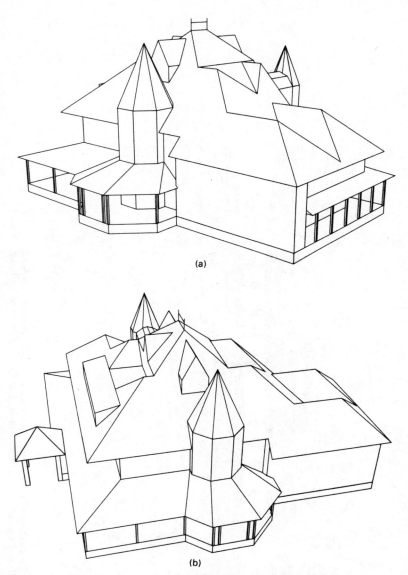

(a)

(b)

Figure 3.2 Exercise 3.1, roof geometries. [*Frank William Andrews House, Middletown, R.I. (1872–1873), by H. H. Richardson*]

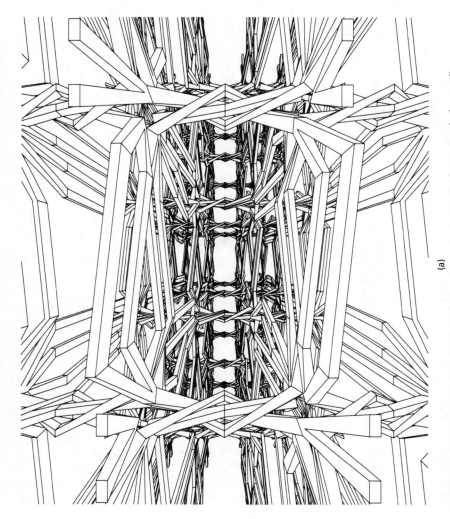

(a)

Figure 3.3 "Perspective of a structure built with a single standard structural element." (*Based on illustrations of Konrad Wachsmann, The Turning Point of Building, Reinhold, 1961.*)

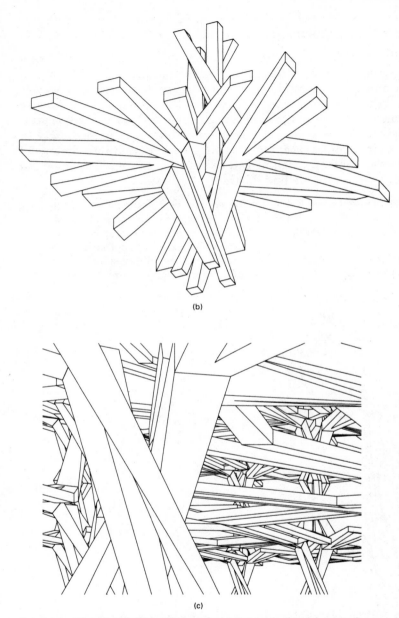

(b)

(c)

Figure 3.3 (*Continued*) "Perspective of a structure built with a single standard structural element." (*Based on illustrations of Konrad Wachsmann,* The Turning Point of Building, *Reinhold, 1961.*)

Exercise 3.3: The Miraculous Mannequin

The ability of CAD to generate a full range of views of the model rapidly is a strong argument for using CAD throughout the design process. The image projected on the monitor has limitations, however. The size of the screen and the uniformity of line weight inhibit a sense of scale and depth. Although plots can be enhanced to reinforce spatial characteristics, design often requires views developed immediately in response to immediate design questions. The insertion into the model of representational scale figures can be valuable in speedily conveying this needed sense of scale and depth.

In the first exercise, a human figure was represented by a single rectangular prism. With the ability to combine planar and curved surfaces, a more representational figure can now be prepared. Figure 3.4 presents a graphic rather than a modeling approach to developing a scale figure. In this instance, a two-dimensional representation of Le Corbusier's "modulor" figure spins around an axis to

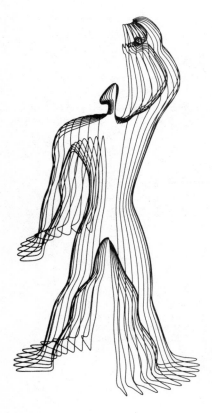

Figure 3.4 Exercise 3.3, The Dancing Modulor.

provide a characteristic shape from many angles. This type of solution is highly memory-intensive. As in any exercise in modeling complex sculptural objects, you will need to abstract the human form into ready-made and custom-made elements. For this exercise, in contrast to the Dancing Modulor, you should design the model to minimize the number of parts while maintaining scale identification. If you have extra time and energy, model an automobile.

Exercise 3.4: Monument to Nature

In the preceding exercises, biomorphic or geometric considerations shaped design ideas. This exercise specifically calls for a sculptural response and employs the full resources of CAD modeling. It explores the interplay between a graphic tool and design imagination; it tests the ability of CAD to communicate complex spatial and volumetric relationships, and it provides an opportunity to experiment with a working procedure involving CAD modeling, drawing, and traditional model building.

The New York City Parks Department has invited you to design a monument to be placed in a clearing in Central Park in close proximity to the Museum of Natural History and the Planetarium. This Monument to Nature is intended to enhance an awareness of natural forces through its form, materials, and construction. While not indicating specific seasons and dates, it should evidence the rotation of the earth on axis and orbit. The shape and location of shadows should mark time. The silhouette of monument against the sky should intensify an awareness of the momentary quality of its light and color. Rain, snow, and sleet should positively interact with the monument. During rainstorms, the monument should become a fountain.

4

Collective Action

Introduction

Beyond its ability to record architectural ideas, the CAD model can itself be thought of as a productive environment for design experimentation. Elements can be defined flexibly and be superimposed quickly in alternative compositions. Component elements can be reconsidered and instantly replaced. Systematic and random processes can be called upon to generate possibilities at every scale of the project.

Among the most useful of CAD's features is its ability to form complex objects from separate graphic elements. This permits the crucial translation in focus from lines and surfaces to real-world analogs. These collective elements, usually referred to as groups or blocks, can themselves be combined into more comprehensive units to eventually build the project model.

Like any design medium, CAD modeling calls for abstraction. Before initiating a new project, it is useful to decide on an overall modeling strategy. Program-generated volumes and surfaces can be used for sketch models. As detailed ideas develop, these initial elements require more complete representation.

Model components, even at a schematic level, can be saved as part of a planning library. These elements can be called upon to facilitate initial design efforts. Other libraries, of increasingly specific building elements, can be developed to correspond with increasingly detailed work. If possible, planning elements should be thought of in generic terms. For example, rather than work with doors of every size and shape, a unit door (1' high with a 1' swing) can be saved. It can be incorporated in future models and dimensioned as required. As the model becomes more representational, planning elements can be replaced by correspondingly more detailed components.

The tendency to associate separate elements into increasingly larger collective units is one of the most basic design operations. A brick forms part of a course to form a wall to enclose a wing, and so on. In architecture, the autonomy of the individual object is exchanged for a contributing role in an expressive order of objects.

The same logic can be applied to modeling. Collective objects formed of elementary graphic components function as a single object. In turn, several groups can be combined to form new groups. This hierarchical nesting of groups can ultimately account for every component of the computer model and every physical object in the projected design.

The direct relation between formal hierarchies and model structure provides a intuitively comfortable environment for design. The modification of any design component automatically affects subsidiary elements. The process of readjusting smaller-scale components as a result of larger-scale changes and the modification of larger-scale elements through the refinement of small-scale elements is essential to modeling and design. When an arcade is moved, each column is relocated. When bays are reproportioned, columns are redimensioned.

This hierarchical organization assists the designer in dealing with the complexity of an increasingly detailed model. Such an ability to maintain a single ordering system for both the design project and the model strengthens the capacity to transform new ideas into alternative possibilities and may result in a clarity of expression in the final project.

Model Management

The use of a 3D CAD model as the central working environment for architectural design makes the entire project available in one integrated representation. However, as the level of detail of a design project increases, this very completeness makes the model difficult to read and therefore difficult to modify. Subsets and groups can be used to isolate relevant portions of the model for study and change.

The freedom to isolate a section of the model, whether it be a region or a formal component, permits a more detached study with all the resources of 3D CAD visualization. The reincorporation of revised components into an unchanged context stimulates reevaluation of both component and context. In structuring the model as a nested group, the design project begins to resemble a Russian doll: one design challenge contains another. By working with nested groups, a traditional strategy for organizing a complex design effort is given an overall discipline.

Although the specific location, shape, and number of project elements may change dramatically through the design process, it is likely that the hierarchical structure will remain substantially un-changed. Flexibility is reinforced by the opportunity to define new groups on an ad hoc basis.[1] These temporary collections can be examined, reorganized, and reintegrated into their preceding groups.[2]

In planning the hierarchical structure of the model, it might be useful to define three levels of composite objects. The total model could be divided into major planning components defined by programmatic relationships. At an intermediate level, groups could consist of systems of repetitive elements. At its least inclusive, groups could contain individual solid objects defined by surfaces or integrated assemblies of such objects.

Group Functions and Design Thinking

The benefits of organizing the CAD model into groups becomes most apparent in developing an initial design concept. Groups can conveniently be defined on the basis of formal and functional relationships. This encourages a logical ordering of the design elements independent of their final location in the project. A carefully planned group structure gives the designer great flexibility in generating alternative compositions. At the same time, the designer retains the ability to redefine subordinate elements in relation to their evolving contexts.

With an organized system of composite objects, the designer has efficient and effective control over the elements of the most complex models. To aid this clarity, a naming system should be developed at the beginning of the model to identify new groups and recall old ones. Since composite objects may be saved independent of the model, names chosen in the context of one project should make sense in others. One approach to such a system can be found in Appendix A.

CAD programs often contain features which allow you to review your catalog of groups and library files, but it is useful to keep an independent record of group names as well as subset definitions and useful viewing coordinates. Initially, these notes may be unsystematic; they will provide an overview of your modeling style. They can assist you in developing a comprehensive system which can be maintained from one project to another.

Introduction to Construction Exercises

The exercises in this chapter were developed to illustrate three ways in which group operations reinforce basic design procedures and attitudes. In Exercise 4.1, a basic formal concept is analyzed and represented. Group operations are used to generate alternative juxtapositions of the elements of the original concept. In Exercise 4.2, specific local forms will be derived from the interplay of project-wide patterns. Exercise 4.3 follows a traditional methodology of developing a project incrementally, from part to whole.[3]

Exercise 4.1: Idea Regeneration

Architectural composition is based on division and association. A complex building program is structured into a limited number of significant elements. These elements are related in a way that both enhances individual identity and projects a collective identity.

CAD modeling provides an excellent opportunity for brainstorming. Often, compositional possibilities are never suggested, let alone drawn, or are excluded as obviously unfit before they have been fully considered. In this exercise, accidental juxtapositions of design elements will be examined for valid and possibly unsuspected alternatives. This procedure takes advantage of the computer's willingness to copy a shape any number of times. The separation of evaluation from idea generation may result in surprisingly interesting possibilities. This exercise is intended as a demonstration of both the flexibility of a hierarchically ordered model and the usefulness of CAD to expand design material.

For purposes of discussion, I will be referring to the series of public libraries designed by H. H. Richardson beginning in 1877. These projects provide an excellent example of the range of possibilities available by exploring alternative compositions of a limited but distinctive group of elements. This exercise will reflect that design procedure by applying CAD capabilities. Use a sketch model of one of your own projects as the basis for a series of transformations. Select a project of some complexity to make the exercise interesting.

The Howard Memorial Library in New Orleans, built after Richardson's death, is illustrated in Figure 4.1. It contains the characteristic elements of the series. The reading room consists of a major space with book-lined alcoves suggesting three levels of nesting. The lowest level of the hierarchy would include groups representing shelves, tables, and walls. These elements would be included in a group representing the typical alcove. The reading room, at the highest level of hierarchy, would include the alcove groups. One could extend this process infinitely in either direction, but for our purposes it will be necessary to work with only three levels.

The complete structuring of a model into nested objects will require the definition of many collective objects. In this exercise, as in any future work, it is useful to develop a system for naming collec-

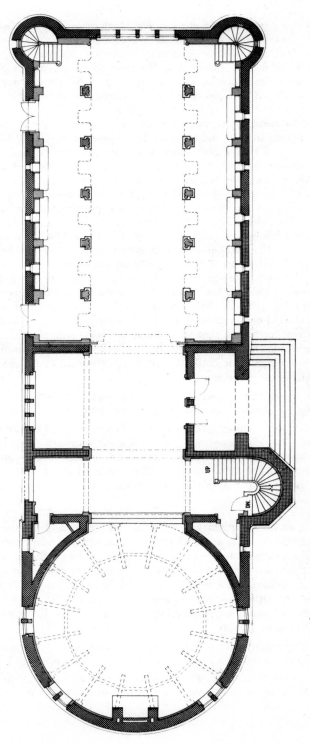

Figure 4.1 Howard Library, New Orleans (1889, op. post.) by H. H. Richardson. (*Courtesy of Errol Barron/Michael Toups, Architects.*)

tive objects. As the number of these elements increases, such a system facilitates element selection and identification.

For this exercise, a seven-character system is suggested. If the structure is seen as a family tree, the first three characters could identify the primary level of components (e.g., ENT for entrance or STK for stacks—if H. H. were to have followed that procedure). The fifth character could be a number to represent the generation of the part, and the final three characters could identify the part. Consequently, a shelf in the reading room could be named RRM3SLF. If your program allows more characters, you can avoid overabbreviation. Maintaining the same number of characters for each component allows the list of names to be sorted more easily.[4]

In building the model of your project, it might be easier to begin at an intermediate scale, develop the overall configuration, and then introduce finer detail. You may decide to fully model only one branch of the hierarchy while sketching out others. Once the model is roughed out, the real benefits of its group organization can be enjoyed. Before getting involved in the main experiment, work with the nested structure of the model on your own. Revisit interesting but rejected organizations. Radically reorganize a subcomponent and examine the impact of the change on the overall scheme.

Compositional elements will be recombined by using a mathematically neutral technique that will generate a wide range of accidental combinations. Since compound objects being randomly combined retain their integrity, it is likely that any juxtaposition of these elements will make some sense.[5]

1. Starting with the original configuration, make a minimum 7 × 7 rectangular array of each of the primary elements.

2. Use a random number generator to determine the horizontal and vertical distances between copies of the same group.[6] To ensure that resulting clusters of groups are a reasonable distance apart, multiply each random number by 2 times the largest dimension of the group. You may also wish to rotate each new array by an angle randomly determined.

Depending on the complexity of the model, the resulting file will be sizable. You can quickly erase all isolated components, combinations which make no sense, and repetitions of the same composition. Some accidental juxtapositions will make diagrammatic sense but may not work in context. Some may be familiar; these you may have considered earlier. Others—and they are the ones in which we are most interested—will make surprising sense or may suggest further possibilities. Figures 4.2a to c symbolize such a process.

3. Select three distinctly different schemes and repeat the process while working with groups that are of a lower hierarchical level.

4. Separate a copy of the most completely modeled primary element from the other models. Break the component down into its subor-

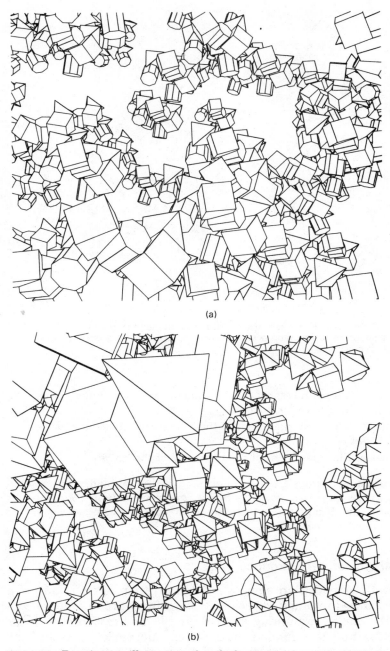

(a)

(b)

Figure 4.2 Exercise 4.1, illustration of method using random arrays (tetrahedrons, cubes, and octagonal prisms represent elements of the original composition).

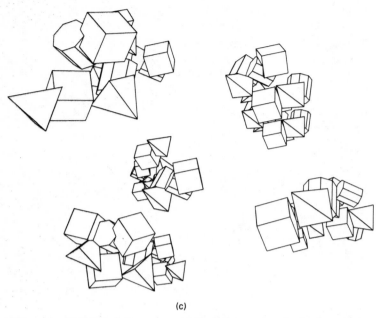

(c)

Figure 4.2 (*Continued*) Exercise 4.1, illustration of method using random arrays (tetrahedrons, cubes, and octagonal prisms represent elements of the original composition).

dinate groups and repeat the superimposed array technique to develop alternative components.

5. Replace the most interesting of the recomposed elements into the first set of solutions.

6. Repeat the experiment at the third step of the hierarchy.

At each scale, arrays are distributed on a horizontal plane. As a result, there may be a tendency to see this exercise as purely two-dimensional. It might be interesting to introduce three-dimensional rotation to the recipe.

Copy, Modify, and Reintroduce

Exercise 4.1 provided an elaborate demonstration of the value of a model organized into nested groups. Separating a group from its context in the model, examining and revising it, and returning it to its original location is a fundamental design and modeling technique. Previously, the group was relocated horizontally. It could equally have been placed on a separate subset and isolated by turning off all the other subsets.[7]

Although the model may be strictly organized into nested groups, it may be necessary to bring together elements from separate groups. For example, in the Richardson library, the major subsystems were planning units. A project-wide examination of structure might be valuable. Modified components can be returned to their original groups. Although this operation may seem overly fussy, the model's hierarchical structure is worth maintaining because it provides flexibility and access.

Experimentation

The following exercises examine two contrasting design processes. Exercise 4.2 calls for incremental development. Simple small-scale elements will be combined to form increasingly specialized assemblies. Exercise 4.3 calls for the translation of programmatic and contextual factors into three-dimensional patterns. The project will develop as a response to these project-wide systems.

The pencil sketch and the 3D mock-up have complementary roles in stating initial design ideas. The sketch conveys an overall impression gradually supported by detail. Early CAD models display the fundamental geometries of an idea. These geometries often involve the repetition and modification of simple spatial units. The units can be modeled with increasing detail, and, as collective objects, they can be copied, rotated, and mirrored to form a series of test models quickly. Unlike the sketch, with its unchanging viewpoint, the sketch model permits flexible observation and recombination that invites further speculation and experimentation.

As models become more complete and the database becomes more extensive, some CAD operations slow down. With planning, you can keep a working database as small as possible until the full complexity of the model is specifically called for. At that point, the full model can be easily assembled. I will discuss one technique for accomplishing this in Chapter 5. In the meantime, every time you consider developing two- and three-dimensional arrays, remember that pans, zooms, and regenerations take much longer and hidden-line operations take significantly longer. Even with the speediest machines, computer intensive operations interrupt the flow of thought.

Exercise 4.2: Nested Groups

CAD modeling favors incremental action. The careful organization of the model can lead to a flexible design approach that is less dependent on the appearance of the groups themselves and more responsive to program and context. An experienced designer uses a range of techniques to help define the nature of the design problem while inviting the generation of a full range of solutions. This exercise looks at one technique reinforced by the qualities of the CAD model. The process begins with the design of subordinate components to the definition of larger-scale relationships.

As an illustration of this technique, three houses will be placed on a sloping site. Initially, the houses will be represented as elemental volumes. They will increase in complexity and detail in response to design opportunities. By carefully coordinating the use of groups, subordinate elements will be modified for a single application or can replace earlier versions throughout the model. The impact of these changes will immediately be tested at each scale.

This procedure relates closely to the experience of working with chipboard study models. Simplified volumes are arranged to better understand site conditions and define an overall approach. The CAD model facilitates the storage of and comparison between alternate solutions. The automatic updating of the entire model as details are modified invites experimentation at a broad range of scales. Although the CAD model does not have the direct physical impact of a chipboard model, its ease of combination and recombination and the reusable record of alternative ideas support imaginative thinking.

Clustered development

This exercise is in three stages. Initially, a schematic house will be modeled as a collection of rooms. Rooms of different sizes and proportions will be scaled from a prototypical unit. Copies of the original house will be positioned on the site. The introduction of site circulation, the modification of each house to respond to specific site characteristics, and the detailed fitting of house and contours will follow. Three-dimensional thinking and the flexibility of CAD modeling will be tested by these adjustments. Finally, one of the three houses will be more fully elaborated. Group copy commands will be used to test the application of these details to the other houses.[8]

> In preparation for designing houses and organizing them on a sloping site, it is useful to define a flexible kit of parts. These few components should be designed to combine in the widest variety of ways while being specific enough to suggest character. Happily, it is always possible to revise and add new elements at any stage.
>
> For schematic purposes, model a series of space-enclosing and structural units useful in sketching a general massing scheme. Instead of directly modeling components with final dimensions, model

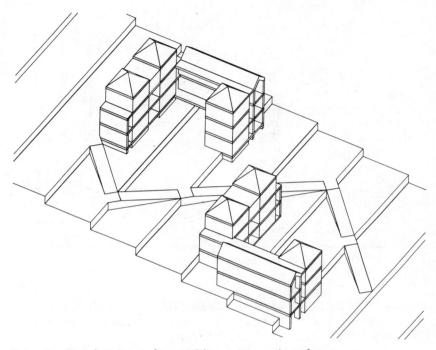

Figure 4.3   Site planning study: repetitive contour, unit, and ramp.

prototypical elements with unit dimensions. When they are introduced into the model, they can be scaled to their specific use. In this
instance, begin with the following elemental components:

1. Unit slab

2. Unit wall

3. Unit roof

4. Unit stair

As the model develops, alternative units will be supplied; they will
be responsive to site opportunities and evolving design ideas. Initially, limit horizontal and vertical dimensions to facilitate combinations. Gradually, the range of possible dimensions can be increased by using scale commands and by modeling new components.

The site

As in the development of the schematic houses, the site can be built up
from elementary units. These pieces can eventually be adjusted and
relocated, simulating cut-and-fill. For our purposes, the site elevation
decreases 50′ from an access road on the west property line to a beach

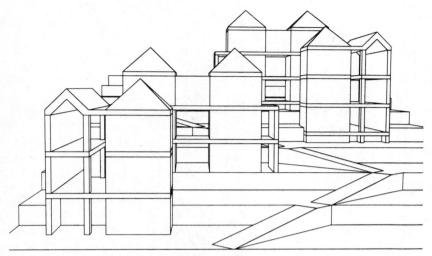

Figure 4.4   Site planning study: view upslope.

to the east. The rectangular site measures 150′ in a north-south direction and 200′ in an east-west direction. Any irregularities in the contours can be overlooked in this initial effort.

The site could be modeled as a collection of unit steps 4′ wide with a 12′ tread and a 3′ riser. The 3′ vertical module is small enough to combine to produce a variety of changes of level and is itself sufficient to have a significant spatial impact. This site might be thought of as a miniature Machu Picchu. Naturally, in later design stages the 3′ contours could be replaced by closer approximations of actual site conditions.

To keep the focus on modeling techniques, all site circulation is pedestrian. Cars are parked directly off the access road along the west property line. Each unit has access to the beach directly from private open space or by means of a common walkway.

Basic circulation elements should be modeled. These component units could consist of the following:

1. Path perpendicular to contours (ramp or stairs represented by a ramp)

2. Path parallel to contours

3. Path diagonal to contours

At first, ignore transitions between these circulation elements and the units themselves. Use color to distinguish circulation from contours and houses.

Unit design

Make general site-planning assumptions to prepare a sketch model of a prototypical unit. The unit should be built from subsidiary groups to facilitate changes. Place three copies of the unit at tentative locations on the site. Recompose and reposition each unit to strengthen site relationships and individual unit designs.

This experience should point out the value of a flexibly organized prototype in encouraging solutions responsive to specific site conditions. For example, the southernmost unit could be organized around a series of south-facing terraces. The association of interior space and adjacent terrace might influence thinking in the other units with less private southern exposure.

> As units become more detailed, elements generated in one model can be tested in the others. CAD modeling encourages this experimentation. Groups can be exploded, edited, and redefined. They can be automatically substituted for earlier versions throughout the model. Less drastically, the new groups can individually replace previous components.
>
> Although orthogonal and parallel projections will be fundamental to model construction, perspectives will establish and confirm major design decisions. Views of the lake from terraces, relationships between interior and exterior spaces, and entrance sequences can be understood only in perspective. Subsets can be selected to filter out information not immediately relevant, and hidden-line views can be developed efficiently. The convenience of viewing the model from new directions and distances reveals unsuspected possibilities. Since these images are unanticipated, they can more easily stimulate the imagination and lead to stronger design concepts.

Since the model is structured by using nested objects, the feedback provided by 3D CAD visualization tools should be more easily translated into new design action. The time initially invested in structuring the model will provide a flexible design environment throughout the project's evolution.

Working from the General to the Particular

In Exercise 4.1, CAD's ability to organize models into groups was used to expand design material. In this project, the same ability will be used to help initiate basic design concepts. Building design will be approached as a response to the interaction of separate organizational systems. The method is similar to jazz: Players respond sensitively to one another; the players are united by a common sense of purpose. The resulting expression is a result of the simultaneous actions of all of the participants. Since project-wide forces combine in locally explicit

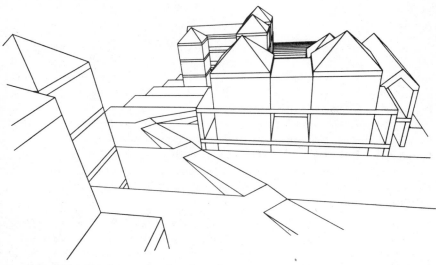

Figure 4.5   Site planning study: view downslope.

ways, there are opportunities to use common elements responsively along with unique elements.

This attention to the unique situation can be balanced by the development of a common architectural vocabulary applicable throughout the project. Modifications can be made to a single copy of the group or to the entire series. Through changes in scale and proportion and through the addition or removal of parts, one architectural element can form the basis of a family of related elements. The organization of the model into groups gives the designer the capacity to enter into an effective dialog with a complex project involving decisions at every scale.[9]

Exercise 4.3: Ferrissopolis

In 1916, New York City introduced new zoning regulations in response to the increasing density of skyscrapers. Setbacks were called for to assure minimum standards of light and air. In the 1920s Hugh Ferriss demonstrated, through a series of dramatic renderings, the potential for translating these requirements into buildings and spaces of power and intensity. As an exploration of the resourcefulness of CAD modeling and group functions, it would be interesting to retrace Ferriss's path and translate systematic requirements into specific forms.

Figure 4.6 Hugh Ferriss, *Zoning Envelopes, 1922: First stage.* (*Reprinted in Jean Ferriss Leich*, Architectural Visions, the Drawings of High Ferriss,*Whitney Library of Design, 1980.*)

In this experiment, dense urban development will be generated by four major factors: circulation, light, climate, and view. Each of these determinants will be translated into a system of regular geometric envelopes and will be represented in CAD terms as groups. Each system will repeat in a regular pattern. As the four systems interact, their correspondences and collisions will begin to suggest opportunities for developing significant and characterful places. An overall formal structure will result from the interweaving of repetitive factors and unique incidents.

The three-dimensional characteristics of each system in terms of distances and frequencies of elements will be described. In each instance, model each system component as a group. As in any fabric, the consistency of each network is essential. Each major system should be modeled as a nested group to facilitate later modifications. The most inclusive group of each system should be so designed that it can be repeated in all directions. With a range of space-filling geometries, Ferrissopolis might develop a richness of spatial intersection that Paris might envy.

Circulation

At an overall scale, circulation is the richest three-dimensional design element. In this experiment a regular movement system occurs at three scales: local, district, and regional. At each scale, circulation spaces should be represented as volumes and should be developed into groups.

Local circulation channels serve workplaces and residences. They occur at 60' horizontal and 30' vertical intervals. At the district scale, local channels connect with promenades occurring at 300' intervals. At this scale horizontal elements are connected by vertical circulation towers also at 300' intervals. In addition to pedestrian circulation, these channels provide access to work centers and commercial facilities and supply services and utilities. These intermedi-

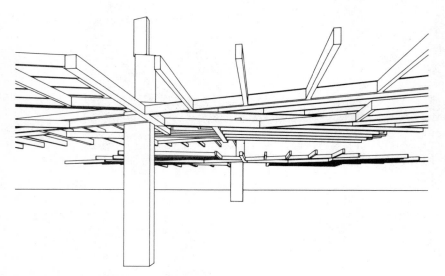

Figure 4.7 Massing study using nested groups: circulation trees.

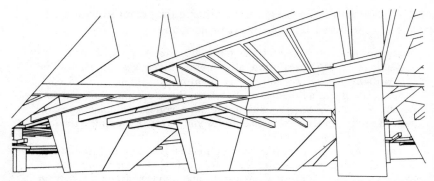

Figure 4.8 Massing study using nested groups: circulation intersected by light courts.

ate paths are open to the sky a minimum of 60 percent of their length. They occur at grade, 90' above grade and 30' below grade. Public transportation intersects the intermediate system every 1500'.

Natural light and ventilation

Open-light courtyards form 30 percent of the development's buildable volume. These conelike volumes are oriented due south, resulting in vertical north walls and 45-degree sloping south walls. They penetrate layers of construction to the ground level and are major sources of daylight and natural ventilation. No working area is to be further than 80' from a courtyard. Prevailing winds travel from west to east. Major public spaces should benefit from natural ventilation, as should work spaces and residences.

Views

In addition to the light courts, public open spaces, amounting to 20 percent of the city's buildable volume, should be provided. Some of these spaces might reinforce points of public transportation access. Others might be considered quiet parks, removed from traffic.

Finally, the statue of Hugh Ferriss has been placed on a 4000'-high cliff overlooking the city he inspired. This statue is located 3 miles due north of the center of Ferrissopolis. In homage to its spiritual founder, the city fathers have ordained that 25 percent of the offices in each building shall have a view of the statue.

None of these specifications are to be taken as serious prescriptions for the ideal city, but they do set up a series of spatial and formal conditions which can be manipulated relative to each other and which could, conceivably, come together in intriguing combinations. The exercise calls for investigation in all projections.

By placing each system on its own graphic subset, it will be easier to experiment with alternative alignments. Each system should be given its own color. By selectively turning subsets on and off, each major system can be studied in isolation. Since each module consists of subordinate elements which are also collective objects, using nested groups in this exercise enables you to modify a single module or the entire system.

Focus particularly on the intersections of systems. In Manhattan, major open spaces occur at the convergence of several movement systems. In Savannah or Charleston, open spaces occur away from movement systems. Given the possible moiré patterns of regularly spaced elements, in and out of phase, a variety of individual episodes will be derived within a consistent overall matrix. Shift the four groups in relation to each other to maximize the repetition of similar conditions. Save this model as 4EX3A. Shift the groups to maximize unique juxtapositions of subsystems. Store this model as 4EX3B.

Choose one of the most interesting regions of either model and introduce enough architectural detail to establish its character. By developing the modules which come into play in the region and their subordinate elements, the entire model will be enriched. By identifying each stage and each alternative version of a component with a coherent group or block name, it is easier to combine a variety of detail solutions.

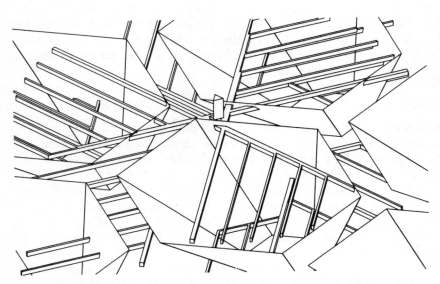

Figure 4.9   Massing study using nested groups: zoning envelopes resulting from interaction of light courts and circulation.

As the model becomes more refined, the number of objects on screen and in the database becomes unmanageable. It is useful to work with two models: one that focuses on overall planning issues and one that concentrates on a specific region. The large model can make use of early schematic versions of repetitive groups; the smaller model can continue to develop more detail.

A model of this density provides ample opportunity to take advantage of the viewing capabilities of CAD. It would be interesting to illustrate the day-to-day routine of an office worker through a series of vignettes. Such a sequence might begin with the most critical and dramatic perspectives of entering a public space from subsurface transportation, approaching circulation towers, and arriving at a desk which looks over the city and the monument beyond.

Notes

1. Microcad programs vary in their method of selecting objects for group formation or other purposes. In some instances, objects must be picked graphically; in others, they can be based on a variety of characteristics (color, subset, line style, and so on).
2. Some CAD programs permit the automatic substitution of a redefined group.
3. As models become more ambitious, frequent backups become essential. There are two degrees of backup: one as part of an archive of significant stages of project development and another to safeguard work in progress. Leaving a clear trail behind allows you to retrace your steps. You can return to an earlier scheme or incorporate more successful parts into the current model.
4. Software varies in its requirements for naming a group. The proposed system is general enough and sufficiently detailed for this exercise. Suggestions for an open-ended naming system are welcomed.
5. You might wish to rotate one or more of the arrays.
6. If you lack a random number generator, the last four digits of any column of telephone numbers will work nicely.
7. An overall approach to working with subsets will be presented in the next chapter. The use of subsets in conjunction with groups is a powerful tool for managing complex models.
8. A convenient naming system for collective objects helps speed up object selection or insertion into the model. In the following exercises, since the collective objects will themselves be evolving, include in each name an indication of version number. Preceding stages in the development of a component can then be more easily retrieved for reevaluation. Earlier and less-detailed components can be substituted for later and more fully elaborated ones, thereby simplifying selected aspects of the model in large-scale views.
9. Note the use of columns in Michelangelo's facades of the Capitoline Museum and Conservator's Palace to frame ground floor openings, to frame second-story windows, and to form balustrades.

Graphic Subsets

Introduction

Full realization of the design potential of 3D CAD depends on the incorporation of groups and subsets into one's modeling technique. The focus of this chapter is on the use of subsets to limit the display to only the aspects of the model that are of immediate interest. By establishing convenient subsets, projections, and views, the designer has precise control over the model's display. This ability to alternate views and imaginatively isolate and juxtapose segments of the model helps in the identification design conflicts and opportunities.

The impact of large-scale decisions on small regions of a project can often be lost in 2D-oriented graphic systems. As design projects have grown in scale, our inability to bring large- and small-scale concerns into harmony has produced a disjointed and disconnected architecture. The three-dimensional consistency of the CAD design model permits an examination of the entire project at a full range of scales. The availability of visualization tools from choice of projection to selection of subsets along with rendering routines provides a preview of the overall concept and detail realization.

Working with a CAD model throughout the design process eventually presents problems of legibility. In early stages, the use of color to identify building systems, along with selective pans and zooms, is sufficient. Since model components multiply like rabbits, however, 3D CAD programs allow you to segment the overall model into subsets. These subordinate models, organized at the designer's convenience, can be displayed in any number of useful combinations.

So far, subsets have been discussed primarily in terms of inspecting the model, but they are as useful in the construction and modification of the model. Coordinating groups with subsets permits the designer to identify, modify, and replace specific sections of the model without disturbing the rest of the model. Collections of model elements can be copied to a temporary subset, placed in a relevant context, revised, and substituted for the earlier components.

Although new subsets can be improvised during the course of the modeling, it is useful to organize a system of subsets before starting. By anticipating future modeling needs, each new object can be assigned to a convenient subset as it is generated. When subset names are easily identified, dimensional guides, diagrammatic sketches, schematic elements, well-defined building-systems, and so on, can be displayed or concealed. A good mnemonic system of subsets allows the designer to quickly get to the elements of the model of most immediate importance.

In the following exercises, I will present a single general strategy for organizing groups and subsets. Each project will call for its own variation of the basic scheme. Individual CAD packages vary in their manner of naming subsets. For example, VersaCAD uses numbers, whereas AutoCAD allows letters and numbers. In all cases, the same strategy applies. Subset and group names should be easy to remember and be immediately associated with their contents. Since this model is organized for design purposes, it will undoubtedly contain alternative versions of project elements. For that reason, subset and group names should indicate a version number. Each system should anticipate eventual requirements but must be open enough to allow additions and modifications. Fortunately, CAD programs allow subset and group names to be redefined at any stage of the model's development.

Using the CAD model as a design tool calls for an organization different in nature from one useful for developing production or presentation drawings. CAD drafting makes use of subsets based on the conventions of production drawings. This order develops from a vertical sequence of plan views. Overall model conventions may develop, but as an exploratory instrument, the CAD design model calls for a project-specific approach. At the same time, a well-organized design model should facilitate the development of working drawings.

The following outline is intended to suggest such a basic organization. Subsets can be divided into four main categories:

1. Planning data
   a. Site information
   b. Use requirements
   c. Environmental factors
2. Design research
   a. Site relationships
   b. Massing studies
   c. Component development

3. Project-wide systems
   a. Structural
   b. Mechanical
   c. Electrical
   d. Floors
   e. Walls
4. Location-related material
   a. Activity-oriented
   b. Spatially-oriented

With an equivalent organization of subsets, component models can be displayed to allow concentration on:

1. Overall massing study by displaying only the subsets containing exterior walls and roof. Other subsets can be displayed to present site-planning information.
2. A major interior space by displaying or eliminating walls, ceilings, and floor to provide an uninterrupted view inside.
3. Exterior elevations by displaying only the subsets which contain elements which affect the exterior form. (Be sure to eliminate interior subsets before requesting a hidden-line drawing.)
4. The complete structural system
5. The circulation system
6. Combinations
   a. Structural plus mechanical
   b. Structure and circulation
   c. Circulation and mechanical
7. A single floor
8. Roof geometries

The use of subsets and groups to display small components of the model independent of their subset assignment is critical as the model becomes more complex. Although objects can occupy only one subset at a time, they can easily be reassigned to a temporary working subset. Consequently, it is possible to isolate local objects from the remainder of the model. Once design questions have been resolved, the objects can be returned to their original subsets. The clarity of your subset system is the most important tool in keeping track of the original locations. If the groups are introduced into the working subset, group names can include subset references.

This shell game requires a definite presence of mind. However, it does provide a secure way to experiment without endangering the entire model. *Warning:* When you are modifying groups, be sure you are viewing all of the affected parts of the model. Before initiating radical changes, be sure you back up. In addition to periodic backups, regularly save copies of your model files to allow you to retrace your steps and access earlier model material for possible use in the current model.

Exercise 5.1: The Villa Rotonda Organized into Subsets

The Villa Rotonda, by Andrea Palladio, is a convenient example to demonstrate the use of subsets and groups. Its multiple symmetries facilitate model building, and its clear organization provides obvious horizontal and vertical divisions. The exercise is in two parts. Initially, one approach to organizing the Villa into subsets and groups will be tested. Once organized, sections of the model will be isolated to permit the improvisation of a set of variations based on Palladio's theme.

A highly simplified model of the Villa Rotonda is sufficient for the purposes of this exercise. Exterior walls and interior walls and floors can be reduced to single planes. Model exterior stairs and porches along with the openings along principal axes. This will provide sufficient detail for the perspectives called for in Exercise 5.2. Our experiments with the Villa Rotonda will be restricted to formal elements.

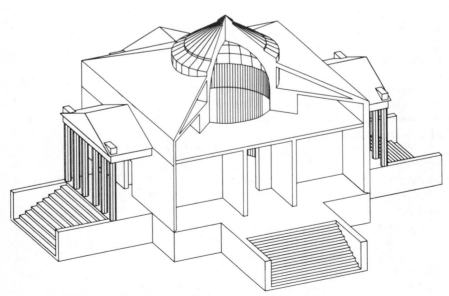

Figure 5.1   Villa Rotonda, façade peeled away.

However, similar procedures could be applied to a more elaborate model. Before proceeding, make sure you have a backup copy of the model.

The 3 × 3 × 3 structure of the Villa Rotonda forms the basis of a subset organization which is described in Table 5.1. The 20 subsets allow great flexibility in isolating and combining model components. To most strongly associate subset names with their content, a consistent naming pattern is used. The first three characters indicate building system, location, and state of completion, in that order. Additional characters, if available, can be used descriptively. If the subsets are well named, the chart, such as that shown in Table 5.1, will quickly become unnecessary.

The advantages of a planned organization of subsets and groups, as developed in the Villa Rotonda model, can be seen in the following shell game demonstration. Since each CAD program handles groups slightly differently, an overall strategy will be described. You may need to modify specific steps.

We will experiment with the proportions of the facades of the Villa Rotonda and the impact of change on the overall volumetric composition. (If one good way to appreciate the elegance of a design is to alter it, electronic modeling provides an innocent way to tamper with this perfection.)

1. Place a copy of the central bay, including portico and exterior stairs, along with one of the adjacent bays of a facade, in subset 00 (previously reserved for experimentation). These components should include model elements located on subsets 10(+), 11(+), 20(+), 21(+), 30(+), 31(+), and 40(+). Turn off all subsets but 00.

2. Working on subset 00, mirror (on a 45° axis) the elements con-

TABLE 5.1 Subset Organization for the Villa Rotonda*

	Ground floor	Main floor	Attic	Roof
Floors	10(+)†	20(+)	30(+)	40(+)
Exterior walls:				
North	11(+)	21(+)	31(+)	
East	12(+)	22(+)	32(+)	
South	13(+)	23(+)	33(+)	
West	14(+)	24(+)	34(+)	
Interior walls	15(+)	25(+)	35(+)	
Temporary subsets	00(+)			

*The true orientation of the Villa Rotonda is northeast-southwest. Accuracy would have added to the confusion.

†(+) is used to indicate additional numbers, letters, and descriptive text if permitted by software.

stituting the side bay to form one corner and define a group out of both sets of elements.

3. Form a second group out of all elements forming the central bay. Basic CAD commands such as SCALE, MIRROR, and ARRAY can be used to reproportion each group and reconstruct the villa.

As proportions change, you will need to realign corners and porticos. Each new version can then be compared to the original along a street of alternatively proportioned Villa Rotondas. Some of the stretched Rotondas may look vaguely familiar (see Figure 5.2). Experiment with round corners and semicircular porticoes.

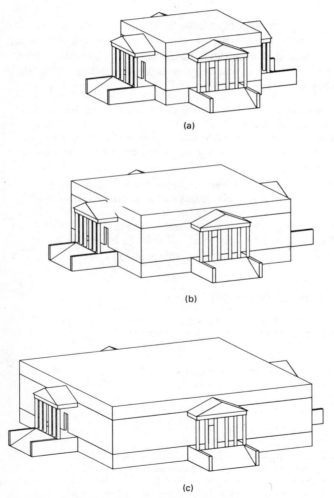

(a)

(b)

(c)

Figure 5.2   Villa Rotonda, proportional distortions.

Exercise 5.2: Subsets and Observation

As demonstrated in Exercise 5.1, subsets permit nondestructive experimentation. A wide range of views of design alternatives can be quickly constructed and saved. The designer can readily switch back and forth from one useful view to another to test new modifications.

A model effectively organized into subsets, in easing the isolation of selected elements, encourages analysis and experimentation. Chapter 6 focuses on the use of the CAD model in design analysis. This exercise demonstrates the use of subsets and groups in examining formal relationships.

1. To speed up regenerations and hidden-line views, isolate the rotunda itself along with the dome and one facade by turning the appropriate subsets on and off.

2. Develop a series of critical perspectives approaching the villa on axis from the garden, including views from the foot of a stair, from the portico through the villa, and finally out the opposite portico back into the landscape. Additional views should explore the rotunda, itself.

3. Select the view in which the dome is almost eclipsed by the front facade. At what distance do you lose sight of the dome? At what point does the surface of the inner dome appear? To what extent are you aware of the soffit of the portico as you climb the stair?

4. Add side elevations to the model. At what distance do you lose sight of the two side porticoes?

5. Since an accurate model of the Villa has been saved to disk, one can feel safe improvising with Palladio's composition. While using subsets to isolate elements under analysis and groups to modify large segments of the model, experiment with reversing major compositional relationships (four rotundas surrounding a cubic room, and so on). The sequence of entrance perspectives could be repeated with larger or smaller rotundas and porticoes to compare variations in quality.

Exercise 5.3: Subsets and Invention

As Exercise 5.2 has demonstrated, subset operations provide a convenient tool for sorting out segments of the model for evaluation and revision. This exercise will look at the use of subsets in the initial design process and through the transition into design development. A provisional organization of subsets and groups will be applied to a project of your own. As the project evolves, this scheme will be adapted to your specific needs. Based on this experience, you will be able to define a framework of subsets and groups more suited to your own design methods.

This exercise demonstrates the integration of all of the modeling skills discussed into an effective design process. Please supply the program and the site of a current or earlier project. To fully test the capabilities of the CAD-modeling environment, the project should be demanding in both organizational and expressive terms.

Eventually the origin (0,0,0) should be located to simplify the accurate placement of objects and groups, but at early stages relating it to site boundaries may be more convenient. Object colors should be chosen to distinguish fixed elements (e.g., property lines) from diagrams and model components. A system for defining and naming groups and subsets should be established. As the design project develops, these initial decisions can easily be revised. An organized CAD model is always more convenient to work with. Initial planning will ensure a comfortable relationship between the evolving structure of model and the project.

Subset organization

Subsets should contain objects most frequently viewed together. Each subset should be descriptively and economically named. Industry-wide standard subset designations are being developed, but it is likely that you will prefer an approach closely related to your design method. In later stages of the project, when it becomes important to interface with other organizations, subsets can be renamed and reorganized.

In the following scheme, three characteristics are indicated in each subset name: location, major building system, and object status. Depending on the nature of the design project, the model could be subdivided into useful regions in a number of ways. Traditionally, horizontal slices have been basic to design and production, but they are not necessarily the most effective ordering system. Major spaces may require their own subsets. Wings, towers, or other vertical sections may need to be isolated.

The accompanying tables illustrate the application of this approach to the preliminary design of a five-story building with a principal space. Table 5.2 takes advantage of each of three digits to indicate a subset's contents. Reading from right to left, each number indicates location (in this instance floor), building system and status. Table 5.3 represents the same organization in alphanumeric terms. With the opportunity of longer names and more characters in subset names there is a temptation to become too specific and literal. As with a numerical system, a consistent shorthand, once assimilated, is easier to work with and takes advantage of wildcard characters (? and *) to access groups of subsets. Adapt this approach to the needs of your project.

Basic system of subsets

Following the organization suggested in Tables 5.2 and 5.3, it is possible to quickly isolate the aspects of a complex model that are of immediate interest. To display a structure three-dimensionally, switch off all subsets. Depending upon your software, turn on all subsets with names ending in 8, 9, and 0 or SH, SV, and FL. Assuming you are about to modify the structural organization, all of the objects displayed would be in subsets 0?? or 0?__??. Alternative components and configurations could be placed in subsets 1?? and 1?__??. Once variations are tested and coordinated with other building systems and revised, they can graduate into subsets 2?? and 2?__??. With each new design cycle, initiated as a new file, all objects with the highest status will be demoted.

The model can be thought of as a stage set. Flats and props can be called up as needed, and objects of little immediate value can be made to disappear. Exterior perspective studies are more efficient if you display only the components of the model that would be visible. Subsets containing elements blocking views of interior spaces can be turned off. With a concise and easily remembered subset organization, the full graphic resources of the CAD model can be quickly accessible.

Color and Collective Object Formation

In addition to its subset designation, each object can be given a number of other characteristics that are useful in forming collective objects. Properties such as line style and line weight have little graphic impact on the model as displayed. With planning, they can simplify the process of pulling together copies of interrelated model components on working subsets for study and development.

Color should be used diagrammatically to identify building systems. That is particularly helpful when several subsets are viewed simultaneously. Color can also be used to identify provisional elements. Temporary jigs or props can be given dark colors in contrast to the lighter colors of the emerging finished objects. Since groups can be defined by color, the props can quickly be deleted when they no longer serve a purpose. Color can also be used to distinguish between two versions of the same object.

It may occasionally be necessary to isolate model elements from several subsets. In some instances, software will permit the elements of a subset to have color and line style distinct from those of the other el-

TABLE 5.2   Numeric Subset Assignment

)Location(						)Building system(
59	49	39	29	19	09	Structure horizontal
58	48	38	28	18	08	Structure vertical
57	47	37	27	17	07	Mechanical
56	46	36	26	16	06	Partitions and equipment
55	45	35	25	15	05	Circulation vertical
54	44	34	24	14	04	Elevation west
53	43	33	23	13	03	Elevation south
52	42	32	22	12	02	Elevation east
51	41	31	21	11	01	Elevation north
50	40	30	20	10	00	Floor

Note: Subset designations can be used to classify objects according to the stage of completion of the project. With purely numeric designation, objects placed in subsets 110 through 150 would indicate their experimental nature. Objects placed in subsets 160 through 200 would indicate greater refinement and acceptance. Objects placed in subsets 210 through 250 would be included in the final project.

TABLE 5.3   Alphanumeric Subset Assignment

)Location(						)Building system(
05__SH	04__SH	03__SH	02__SH	01__SH	09__SH	Structure horizontal
05__SV	04__SV	03__SV	02__SV	01__SV	09__SV	Structure vertical
05__ME	04__ME	03__ME	02__ME	01__ME	09__ME	Mechanical
05__PE	04__PE	03__PE	02__PE	01__PE	09__PE	Partitions and equipment
05__CV	04__CV	03__CV	02__CV	01__CV	09__CV	Circulation vertical
05__EW	04__EW	03__EW	02__EW	01__EW	09__EW	Elevation west
05__ES	04__ES	03__ES	02__ES	01__ES	09__ES	Elevation south
05__EE	04__EE	03__EE	02__EE	01__EE	09__EE	Elevation east
05__EN	04__EN	03__EN	02__EN	01__EN	09__EN	Elevation north
05__FL	04__FL	03__FL	02__FL	01__FL	09__FL	Floor

Note: Alphanumeric subset designations allow greater opportunities to indicate the relationship of an object to the stage of completion of the project. In this example, the first character can represent object status.

ements. These attributes can be used to assemble desired elements in a temporary subset. With other programs, it may be necessary to place copies of the desired elements in the subset. In that case, collect all elements which directly interact with the primary space in subset XX. (When groups can trespass subsets, give them a special line style. That will facilitate their later replacement.) Experiment with your software to discover the most convenient method of forming collective objects, defining a new context, modifying them, and reintegrating them into the model.

Diagrammatic Model

Thus the model of constraints can initially be used as a crude map to search for the vantage or starting points most likely to open up the major or central issues. Later the model can also be used as a way to deliberately transport the designer to another part of the forest. Many of the so-called creativity techniques are generalized methods of provoking the mind into looking at a problem from new viewpoints.[1]

Although each designer may begin a project differently, 3D CAD can provide powerful support for early experiments. No matter how flexibly CAD presents design data, knowledge, experience, and imagination are required to uncover inherent possibilities. Once an initial approach is selected, CAD provides a resourceful tool for testing an idea.

Since most parameters are three-dimensional, they can readily be abstracted in model form. Site information such as boundaries, topography, and surrounding structures can be represented. Solar angles can be plotted as geometric volumes. As three-dimensional diagrams variously superimposed, they can reveal possible relationships only indirectly suggested in two-dimensional form.

The placement of such diagrammatic material in reserved subsets makes the subsets accessible throughout the design process. These reference diagrams can be consulted to check the adequacy of sun control devices or the maintenance of view corridors. Although the inherent precision of CAD modeling does not lend itself to sweeping design gestures, essential relationships can be approximated by simple geometric volumes.

As long as traditional graphic techniques are used to complement CAD modeling, the geometrical bias of the computer can be alternated with more organic procedures. Laser-sharp lines of colored light can happily complement sensual strokes of charcoal. The transition from a statement of fundamental relationships to a formal idea of image and identity, although assisted by the clarity of the computer diagram, remains personal. 3D CAD modeling is particularly effective in translating that idea into geometric terms and supporting its continued elaboration.

> The diagrammatic model should be developed within the range of initial subsets. Save the diagrammatic model for eventual comparisons with the evolving model. While referring to the diagrams and working within the experimental subsets, build a mass model of the project. Introduce library elements to provide scale reference and alternate between large- and small-scale design issues. Often, the ideas that evolve eventually may not be applied to the project at hand. Along with components of direct application, you may wish to export the components as additions to an evolving library of ideas.
>
> Provisionally, a set of boxes, cylinders, or spheres can be arranged in the model to provide some dimensional bearings. Locate these reference forms on a dedicated subset. As illustrated in preceding exercises, multiple copies are helpful in quickly suggesting the main volumes of a model. The shell game technique can be used to gradually replace these temporary volumes with more accurately modeled components.

As the design project continues past the conceptual phase, models become more detailed and representational. Depending upon project complexity and system characteristics, the point at which a model becomes unmanageably complex may be reached. It will then be necessary to work with several interrelated models. The nested group concept discussed in Chapter 4 can be applied to such a collection. One model, probably derived from early study models, will include the major components of the project as general masses. Additional models will develop components of this general model in detail. Overall compositional or organizational questions could be resolved with the most generalized models. Critical sections from the more detailed models could be imported to support specific design decisions. Consistent subset and group names facilitate such exchanges. In the rare instances when a fully detailed and complete model is required, it could be assembled from the subordinate models. Highly detailed small-scale components can replace more abstract versions in more-inclusive models.

A well-tempered CAD model, organized into useful subsets and groups, gives the designer access both to small regions of the project and large scale subsystems. Elements deep within the project can be exposed. Objects geographically remote, yet of thematic interest, can be temporarily brought into the design arena. Organizations of elements extending throughout the project can be isolated, facilitating major revisions and minor adjustments. Repetitive details can be reformulated and their overall impact can be seen immediately. The exercises just completed were intended to assist readers in developing a resourceful technique for managing an increasingly complex design model. In Chapter 6, these skills will be applied to the activities of analysis and evaluation.

Note

1. Bryan Lawson, *How Designers Think,* Architectural Press, Ltd., London, 1980, p. 153.

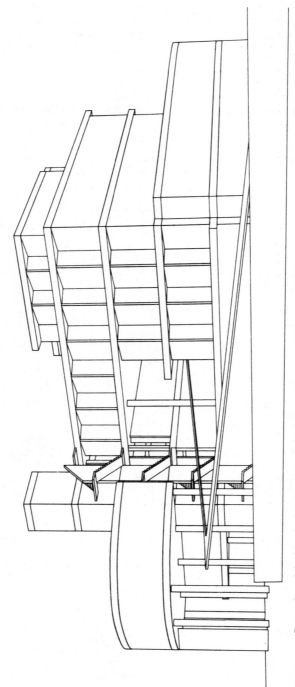

Figure 6.1   General model of Le Corbusier's Carpenter Center, Harvard University (1963).

6

CAD and Analysis

Practical experience had taught him that embryonically all problems contained all answers when one could discover a means of rendering them explicit.
MARSHALL MCLUHAN ON THOMAS A. EDISON[1]

Introduction

In a CAD model used to record and develop project ideas the designer has an excellent tool for investigating program and context. The goal of this chapter is to demonstrate CAD's value in the analysis and evaluation of the design project. Analysis will be discussed as a central design procedure that leads to the clarification and elaboration of design concepts by supporting self-criticism and evaluation. Three-dimensional graphic analysis will be used to express organizational and formal information with accuracy and flexibility.

Analysis is valuable at each stage of the process from early schematic sketches to final documentation. Taking advantage of the properties of CAD modeling, diagrams can be superimposed in any combination and viewed from any angle. This flexibility encourages a deeper understanding of the project and stimulates the generation of more comprehensive design ideas.

The CAD model lends itself to quantitative and visual analysis. Auxiliary programs can be used to examine the CAD database in order to develop estimates of construction cost and evaluate energy efficiency and functional proximity. This chapter emphasizes graphic analysis relying on visual thinking for interpretation and evaluation. Exercises will illustrate the development of analytical models from the design model. In turn, the CAD environment simplifies the modification of the design model in response to the insights gained by such a process.

Graphic Analysis

Visual thinking is central to every aspect of design. Rudolph Arnheim[2] has defined this kind of perception as a fundamental cognitive process that is quite foreign to the computer. However, the juxtaposition of elements developed by a graphic analysis of a design project stimulates the discovery of relationships and possibilities. This partnership between a consistent and flexible three-dimensional representation and design intelligence is a powerful one.

Visual thinking suggests a dialog between conscious and unconscious operations. It brings to bear cultural and historical material. The graphic gesture has always been the architect's link to unconscious thought processes. This route is exemplified by the imprecision of Louis I. Kahn's evocative charcoal sketches for the Kimball Art Museum (Figure 6.2).[3] The dialog between graphic representation and space and volume is a fundamental example of visual thinking and is central to the training of the architect. The possibilities and implications of these lines and shapes are interpreted, evaluated, and acted upon. The resourcefulness of the CAD model adds new possibilities to the visual quality of design thinking.

In preceding chapters, techniques for using CAD modeling to generate and represent ideas have been developed. Analysis was inevitably present as an integral element of design thinking. This discussion explores its value as a specific and independent activity.

Definition

> Essentially analysis is the ordering and structuring of the problem. Synthesis, on the other hand, is characterized by an attempt to move forward and create a response to the problem.[4]

Analysis is a central component in a careful design process. The rigor with which it is carried out varies from architect to architect. Analysis itself is imaginative. Supported by the resourceful use of CAD's flexibility, analysis can take on a more active role in the design process.

Design analysis is based on the application of a general system of categories to a specific case. Analysis breaks down the organic unity of the design project. In so doing, it makes explicit the underlying relationships and assumptions of the current solution.

The goal of analysis is understanding rather than judgment. By allowing a close examination of basic assumptions, vitally different approaches to a problem dealing directly with the fundamental planning and expressive issues of a project can emerge. Once formulated, the

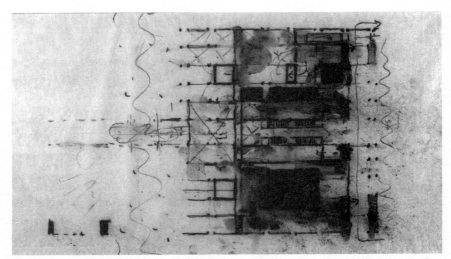

Figure 6.2   Louis I. Kahn, *Study for Kimball Art Museum.* (*From The Louis I. Kahn Collection, University of Pennsylvania and Pennsylvania Historical and Museum Commission*)

analysis can continue to be useful in maintaining a clarity of vision and sense of priorities.

Diagrammatic models can be developed directly from the program and context. Graphic information extracted from the design model must be simplified. The act of abstracting is itself fundamental to design analysis. The process implies a hierarchy of formal relationships in which detail is used to support a larger-scale concept.

By breaking down the complexity of the complete model into three-dimensional analytic diagrams, it becomes possible not only to examine the links within the elements of a category but to discover the relative dependence of one system on another. Resulting changes can be performed on the set of analytical models before revising the design model.

Ideally, evaluation is a separate process based on the analysis. Independent of judgment, the work is strengthened by this clarification. Insights developed by close examination of the project present new opportunities and suggest alternative solutions.

Use of the CAD Model in Analysis

The CAD model lends itself to a broad range of analytical procedures. A flexible and accurate record of the design concept can be maintained continuously through the design process. Its organization into subsets and groups permits the convenient identification and isolation of systems and elements.

Initially, the analytical model consists of a selection of elements of the complete CAD model in accordance with predetermined criteria. Once isolated, these elements are edited to clearly express the organizational and formal idea. This process results in a series of three-dimensional diagrams. These diagrams can be combined or superimposed on the original design model. By examining the diagrammatic models from a variety of viewpoints, a clear understanding of conflicts and possibilities can be developed. The very nature of a flexible three-dimensional presentation of fundamental project information encourages an imaginative spatial and sculptural response. As the value of a CAD-based analytical process becomes recognized, designers will develop their batteries of favorite analytical techniques that can be shared and transferred from project to project. Analytical models can themselves form libraries and be imported into new projects for comparison.

Preceding chapters are concerned with the development and construction of useful design models. This chapter, in contrast, breaks the design model down into separate models representing categories of analysis. Working with the CAD model from the earliest conceptual notions to final documentation has many benefits. Of most immediate interest, project analysis can be richly developed from the CAD model. The model itself is the source of the analytical model. Subsets developed during model construction provide an initial sorting of diagram material. Planes and volumes can be copied to subsets reserved for analysis. The models developed in this manner can be edited to clarify their structure.

In what are probably the most useful analyses, the project is considered from directions distinct from the initial design approach. Although the analysis may be initiated to resolve by a specific issue, it can be purely exploratory. The discovery of analytic approaches will stimulate thinking about future projects.

New subsets should be established for each analytical model. Volumes and surfaces should be copied from the original model, leaving the project model intact. Objects may be incorporated into several analytical models where they will be further edited. Therefore, it is more accurate to derive each model from the original design model.[5]

The set of viewpoints originally used to study the design model may prove convenient for defining useful views of analytical models. A consistent color-coding system also is useful, especially if analytical models of different projects are to be combined and compared. For example, a red circulation system could be dramatically juxtaposed against the black density of the project model.

Methodology

> The mind meets here, at an elementary level, a first instance of the general cognitive problem that arises because everything in this world presents itself in context and is modulated by that context. When the image of an object changes, the observer must know whether the change is due to the object itself or to the context or both, otherwise he understands neither the object nor its surroundings. Intertwined though the two appear, one can attempt to tease them apart, especially by watching the same object in different contexts and the same context acting on different objects.
>
> The object under observation must, then, be abstracted from its context. This can be done in two fundamentally different ways. The observer may wish to peel off the context in order to obtain the object as it is and as it behaves by itself, as though it existed in complete isolation. This may seem to be the only possible way of forming an abstraction. However, the observer may also wish to find out about the object by observing all the changes it undergoes and induces because of its place and function in its setting. Here the abstraction, while singling out the object, does not relinquish the effects of the context but relies on them for an indispensable part of the information. The two procedures serve different purposes, but for both of them it is necessary to tell object and context apart.[6]

Arnheim describes the basic process of analysis as the subtraction of context. The exercises in this chapter will present several examples of using subsets and groups to isolate model components for purposes of analysis.

The convenience of direct visual comparisons between alternative schemes and systems may be CAD's most valuable contribution to analysis. The ability to isolate and superimpose selected model components contributes to a deeper understanding of the underlying structure and principles. These insights lead to solutions that are more comprehensive. At the same time, this systematic view emphasizes an objective and conceptual view of architecture over an experiential one.

There are a variety of approaches to design analysis. The project can be seen as made up of a series of overall systems. For example, such an analysis might isolate the circulation systems, the structural system, and so on. Another approach is to examine patterns of density and frequency rather than function. A third approach is to look at the ordering system itself. It compares the placement of elements in the current project to the original formal diagram.

Such classifications can allow the examination of the project from points of view distinct from the initial design thinking. By providing new perspectives, the original definition of the problem can be expanded and strengthened.

Introduction to Exercises

The following exercises suggest a variety of analyses. To complete them, it is assumed that you have developed a project or are in the process of developing a CAD model of a current project. It is possible to use models developed in preceding chapters, but since there is more at stake and more mystery in current design projects, it seems that the following exercises will be more interesting and useful when applied to a work in progress. In addition to these suggestions, feel free to experiment with your favorite analytical procedures.

Earlier chapters are concerned with constructing and experimenting with models. The scope of the models tends to be restricted to the project itself. Analysis, on the other hand, deals with the project in its larger context as well as its internal configuration. In the same way the designer investigates the larger context in developing the project, design analysis should involve every significant framework. An analytical model may encompass the full scope of the project, or it may focus on smaller sections of the project.

Exercise 6.1: Building-Wide Systems

While working with two alternative schemes of an existing project[7], three building-wide systems will be examined. The analysis will consider structure and surface. Surface will be further divided into exterior and interior components. This separation will permit us to distinguish major interior spaces from exterior mass. The analysis can be extended beyond the building itself to include surfaces defining exterior space. The resulting analytical models will produce a CAD model analogous to the Nolli Map of Rome as reproduced in Figure 6.3.[8]

> The design model's components can be moved or copied to a subset reserved for each analytical category. Ordinarily, the resulting model will be too detailed. It should be edited for diagrammatic clarity. By selecting the appropriate subset, the analytical models can be combined.
>
> The three subsets constituting the analytical model should be exported as a new file. Repeat the procedure with the model of the alternative scheme. Since the two files will be combined, assign different subsets to the second set of models.
>
> Before combining the two files, experiment with each analytical

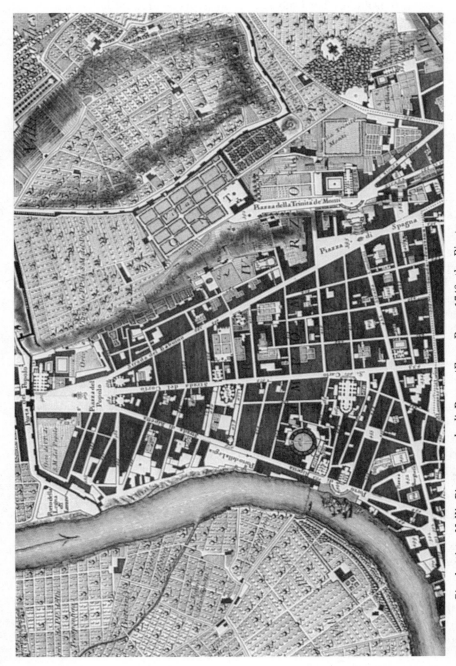

Figure 6.3 Giambattista Nolli, *Pianta grande di Roma. (From Rome 1748: the Pianta grande di Roma of Giambattista Nolli in facsimile; J. H. Aronson, Highmount, N.Y.; 1984)*

model in isolation. Turn subsets on and off to examine an individual system and combination of systems. Experiment with a range of critical views (both three-dimensional and orthogonal) to locate the most revealing ones for comparative analysis. In Figure 6.4, only the subsets of the CAD model of the Carpenter Center containing circulation and site information are presented.

From this initial exploration a number of observations can be made. To what extent does structural organization correspond with exterior volume? What is the relationship between interior spaces and exterior form?

Exercise 6.2: Systematic Views

In the first group of exercises, the analytical categories themselves were emphasized. In this group, we focus on ways of examining analytical models independently of the systems being considered.

Before CAD modeling automated perspective construction, designers tended to choose flattering angles. Since perspectives now require the selection of two points in space and the degree of foreshortening, the designer is free to develop a system of views that represents the project more objectively. Although not all of the views constructed in this manner may be revealing, the views that are not will present useful feedback.

Our purpose is to take a survey of the project by projecting unbiased nonselective views. A grid of views with mathematically determined origins and vantage points will present the model in unexpected ways. Walk-throughs with perspectives constructed at uniform intervals will reveal unexpected relationships. Both systems would be useful if applied to the full design model, approaching the experience of a visitor.

Since the graphic database is consistent, each new perspective displays accurate information. Examining a diagrammatic model clarifies relationships and reveals possibilities overlooked when the more seductive and complex detailed model is examined. The ability to superimpose alternative combinations of systems gives these views additional value. The ability to alternate between the full design model and any juxtaposition of analytic models from the same vantage point can be particularly useful.

Views so developed may eventually be adjusted to clarify key relationships. Refinements, rather than emerging from the prejudices involved in developing the composition, will grow out of a spirit of inquiry rather than justification.

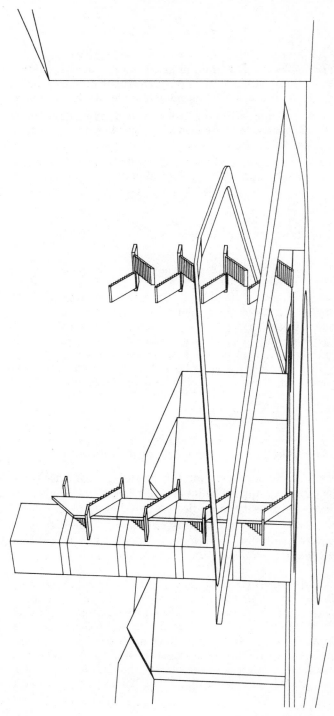

Figure 6.4 Exercise 6.1, analytical diagram of circulation as applied to model of Le Corbusier's Carpenter Center, Harvard University.

Grid of views

1. On a plane perpendicular to the axis of investigation and on a temporary subset, draw a uniform grid. The divisions should be spaced to coincide with or to ignore subdivisions and axes of the model. The intersections of this grid will serve as station points.

2. Corresponding targets will be established by copying this initial grid to the opposite side of the model. Be sure to place the second grid along the axis of investigation.

3. Develop a series of perspectives using the station points and targets established by the two grids. Any adjustments made to viewing distance and angle of view should be maintained throughout the series.

4. By selectively turning subsets on and off, use these views to examine project and diagrammatic models singly and in combination.

Walk-through

CAD modeling programs include or can be supplied with walk-through capabilities. Develop a sequence of perspectives at equal intervals along a designated path.[9] Temporarily, examine the views individually rather than as a sequence. Since these views are developed on a purely mathematical basis, they present the project more neutrally. Once developed, the walk-through perspectives can be used to examine any combination of analytical and design models.

Exercise 6.3: Analysis Based on Density and Distribution

The CAD model can be surveyed for the occurrence of an element of construction or building material. Its regularity or irregularity of distribution, its relative density, may be the by-product of unrelated design decisions. However, the pattern established by the disposition of the elements under study may provide useful and unexpected insights into the project itself.

It is worthwhile to develop a series of analyses for examining factors not directly considered in the organization of the original project. Such inquiries should reveal unexpected characteristics of the project. If these studies prove to be useful, they can form part of a series of standard tests that continue to be applied to new projects.

For example, the locations of corner grocery stores in New Orleans neighborhoods reveal a structure of streets that is important at a neighborhood scale. This structure cannot be understood from a

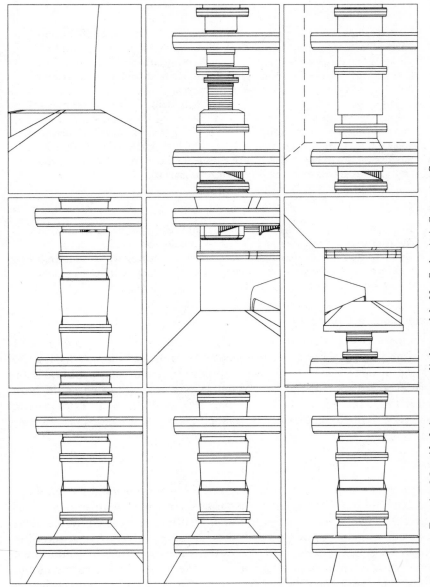

Figure 6.5 Exercise 6.2, grid of views as applied to model of Le Corbusier's Carpenter Center, Harvard University.

street map. The relative density of the groceries reflects economic status, the proximity of supermarkets, and the public transit stops.

Survey of openings

Develop new volumes representing horizontal and vertical openings such as windows, doors, and skylights. Place all horizontal and all vertical openings on separate layers. The isolation of wall and floor penetrations from the complexity of the entire model should present patterns of internal and exterior relationships.

These diagrammatic models should describe patterns of movement and the activity. The relative scale of openings can suggest the distribution of spaces similar in scale. The geometrical relationships between openings may indicate circulation patterns and suggest movement sequences. The relative concentration and depth of exterior openings can describe daylight orientation.

Use of materials

The distribution of a finish material may coincide or conflict with the hierarchical order of spaces. Copy to a separate analytical layer all instances of the use of wood. Timber structure, wood paneling, and built-in cabinets can be combined in the same analytical model if things do not get too confusing.

Additional suggestions

The model's spaces could be identified in terms of their predominant activity. The pattern of seating locations could be compared with the pattern of openings. Locations establishing orientation could be seen in relation to seating and openings. Any zoning concern could be a useful basis for an analytical model. For example, spaces requiring acoustic privacy could be distinguished from noisy spaces.

Exercise 6.4: Formal Analysis

The exercises of the following group are more conventional formal analyses. They emphasize the elements that form the central image of the project envisioned by the designer and, ideally, appreciated by the user. Since CAD models are developed at full scale, analyses from preceding exercises can be superimposed over current material. The coordination of formal with structural, mechanical, and other building-wide systems can be studied. Based on such juxtapositions, the designer can clarify the degree of relative coordination or independence.

Formal analyses seem to grow out of two fundamental attitudes. Building form can be considered a static composition of spaces in con-

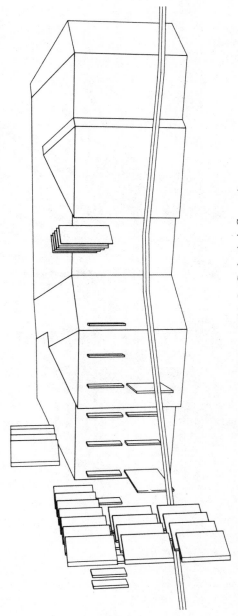

Figure 6.6 Exercise 6.3, analysis of distribution of *brise-soleil* in Le Corbusier's Carpenter Center, Harvard University.

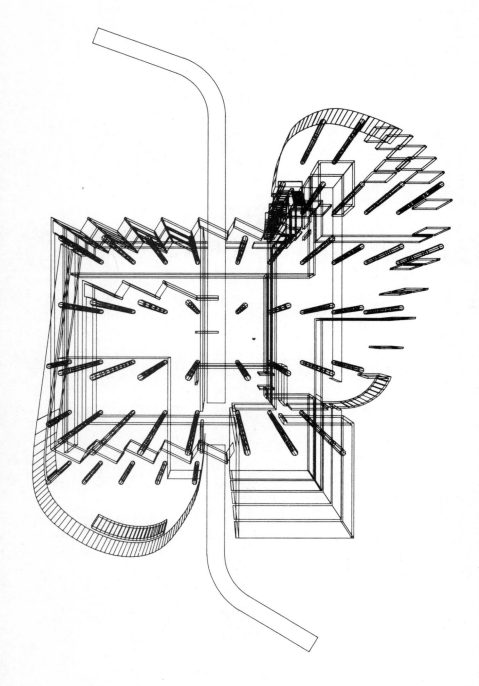

Figure 6.7 Exercise 6.4, analysis of relationship between circulation and principal spaces in the Carpenter Center.

versation laced together by a movement sequence. Alternatively, form can be understood as the result of a compositional act which seeks to communicate its own operation.

Analysis of spatial composition

Copy the surfaces that define the major interior spaces in the project model to a new layer. (Exercise 6.1 can provide some of these components.) Rework the resulting model for diagrammatic clarity. Introduce major horizontal and vertical circulation spaces into the analytical model as a separate subset. After examining each system independently, compare the two organizations. How independent or interdependent is each system?

Form as evolution

This analysis focuses on the dimension of time. A series of analytical models, each representing one stage in the evolution of the composition, can be extracted from the design model. Models representing different stages in the design process should be placed on separate layers. The recreation of the design process, aside from explaining the current project, may be a guide to project interpretation.

Architecture can be understood as an absolute arrangement of forms in equilibrium, or it can be seen as the expression of the interaction of forces. Form may reflect the interaction between ideal formal notions and the specific contextual or programmatic needs. The works of Le Corbusier embody the expression of these conflicts and the act of making architecture. The appreciation of the project can be directly related to the clarity in which its making is communicated.[10]

It would be interesting to combine models representing the design process with those depicting the current organization of structure or circulation. This comparison presents the placement of elements as the consequence of a thought process. Such a procedure invites an evaluation of both the resulting organization and the design process is invited.

Exercise 6.5: New Linkages

In the preceding exercises, objects were selected from the design model and copied to layers representing analytical categories. The analyses were based on building system, dimension, location, and sequence. Other analyses require the expression of intensity or importance[11] and may call for the introduction of graphic codes (hatches, color, and so on). These diagrammatic qualities are, however, still properties of the isolated unit rather than to the association between units.

Using the properties of subsets and nested groups, the analytical model can demonstrate the qualities of independence and flexibility rather than symbolize them. This inquiry can identify the controlling elements and emulate the extent to which they impose limitations on other elements. As opposed to a static visual representation of systems, such an analytical model can emulate the compositional freedom inherent in the program.

In place of a static model of the present composition, this is an active model inviting experimentation and verification. Subsets would contain loose associations of elements, whereas groups would represent a cluster of elements with a fixed geometry. Groups could be moved, rotated, mirrored, and so on. while retaining their essential geometrical order. They could be copied and exploded to form a mutation with similar systematic characteristics yet distinct internal relations (isomerism).

By reconstructing the design model as a game with loosely or rigidly attached pieces, the original path of decisions can be reconstructed. Major alternative strategies can be tested in the light of new understanding. This form of analysis closely relates to the circular nature of the design process. Initial assumptions are ideally based upon the best and most pertinent information available and lead to initial design concepts. Discoveries growing from these first steps raise new questions which further enrich the definition of the design problem. Through such a process, the analytical model can retain its essential characteristics of generating idea and component elements and thereby facilitate experimentation.

Additional Exercises: Variations and Oppositions

The analytical models themselves can be manipulated and recombined to further illuminate characteristics of the project. One way to test an organization is to upset it. By working with one analytical model at a time, the complexities of the full project can be ignored. While focusing exclusively on issues raised by the analytical model, it is possible to rearrange the components of the CAD model to generate new alternatives.

An examination of these choices can renew your understanding of the original decision-making process. Since all the other analytical models are available on other layers, it is possible to combine new diagrams with earlier analyses for further comparison. Perhaps not strictly an analytical technique, working with alternative diagrams is an excellent method for testing basic decisions.

In the extreme, one could take a diagrammatic model and develop its antithesis. A scheme which reverses as many decisions as possible while making use of existing model components can be helpful in understanding the central ideas generating the original concept. If it is questioned in diagrammatic form (with or without additional analytical models), it can be more completely understood and evaluated in a provocative context.

Conclusions

I hope I have been able to demonstrate the utility of CAD modeling as a media for design and analysis. I expect that designing with CAD will suggest techniques and systems related to your own design methods. I suspect that CAD possibilities will lead you to develop new design procedures and, as a result, expand and enrich your architecture. A battery of design techniques and analytical systems can be developed, and they can be applied from one project to another.

Notes

1. Marshall McLuhan, *Understanding Media: The Extensions of Man,* McGraw-Hill, New York, 1964, p. 242.
2. Rudolf Arnheim, *Visual Thinking,* University of California Press, Berkeley, 1969, p. 13. "The cognitive operations called thinking are not the privilege of mental processes above and beyond perception itself. I am referring to such operations as active exploration, selection and synthesis, completion, correction, comparison, problem solving, as well as combining, separating, putting in context."
3. Kahn's charcoal technique reflected a thinking process which moved from uncertainty to clarity, from general notions to specific realizations.
4. Bryan Lawson, *How Designers Think: The Design Process Demystified,* Architectural Press, Ltd., London, 1980, p. 27.
5. It is useful to develop a technique in which you copy objects without changing their location. One copy can be placed on the analytical layer while the other remains a part of the original model. With practice, you will discover the most convenient way to do this with your software.
6. Rudolph Arnheim, op. cit.
7. For this demonstration, you may wish to backtrack to the point when there were competing schemes or reconfigure your current model to construct a worthy alternate. Models prepared for earlier chapters may be used as well.
8. Traditional sources can suggest CAD analyses. With computer modeling they can be fully three-dimensional, they may prove useful in unanticipated ways.
9. When a walk-through feature is not available, construct these views manually. The coordinates of the station point and target point, once established, can be varied consistently. The angle of view will remain constant.
10. Geoffrey H. Baker, *Design Strategies in Architecture: An Approach to the Analysis of Form,* Van Nostrand Reinhold, New York, 1989.
11. Facilities Management software requires the assignment of a degree of importance of the association between two spaces. The goal of the operation is to maximize the proximity of spaces with strong affiliations.

Appendixes

Appendix A: Hierarchical Process

Constructing CAD models requires a major investment of time. Structuring the design and model-building process in a clearly hierarchical fashion can improve your efficiency: It facilitates precise control over the amount of detail displayed on the monitor or in hardcopy output. The fully detailed model can work in conjunction with a second, more diagrammatic model that is perhaps the result of an earlier design stage.

In Chapter 4, nested groups are discussed as devices for placing all of the elements in the model in increasingly inclusive groups. As the model grows in complexity, earlier studies of major building components can be saved in supporting files. 3D models can be developed with a degree of detail that depends on the purpose of the intended output. Access to the fully modeled project and less-elaborated stages allows the designer to combine components of several parallel models specifically for purposes of communication.

The process of translating a fully realized 3D model into useful 2D output is interesting but quite unrelated to the characteristics of the 3D model itself. Fortunately, this process is not difficult and requires a selection of material already developed and edited for clarification. Normal graphic concerns about line weight and line style are ordinarily not issues in model building. Since edges are intended to be seen from a variety of views, they need not be selected individually and be given a unique weight. Hidden lines are not dashed in but disappear behind closer solids. Preparing models for 2D plots often involves opening new files specifically for the plot. Selections from the complete model are copied into the new files and arranged and edited within the context of the intended plot.

Appendix B: File Management Systems

The well-tempered CAD model results from the careful preplanning of the design process and the use of groups and subsets. Additional organization is required to keep track of the files associated with the model. In Appendix A, I discuss the value of a family of related CAD models, each containing less-detailed and more diagrammatic material. This was seen as a resource for determining the amount of detail to be included in a particular exported drawing. Other accompanying files include libraries, earlier versions of a scheme, alternative solutions, diagrammatic material, and so on. Material contained in these files should be available throughout the design process.

A filename should identify the project and the relation of the file to the project. They should be clear enough that they make sense years later. It is possible to develop an index to accompany storage disks of these files with more detailed descriptions but it would be preferable if the role of each file were obvious.

Primary files contain the entire model and should convey the version number. Dependent files should refer to the version of the project they support. Files for export purposes should be easily identified. A sample of scheme (given the eight-character limitations of DOS) could be:

1 2 3 4 5 6 7 8

P R O J 1 A X ?

Character

1–4	PROJ indicates a four-letter project designation
5	Version number
6	Alternative scheme
7	Subordinate file (X = export)
8	Discretionary

Appendix C: Notes to Instructors

Before using this book as a text, students should already have received a basic introduction to CAD which emphasizes the mathematical and geometrical basis of architectural graphics. Since exercises contained in *The CAD Design Studio* should give students the chance to become proficient in the software, students should have an overall sense of the program's command structure (particularly the relationship of 2D and 3D CAD) and should understand the basics of drafting and constructing a simple model. Once such an overview is presented and the student has the confidence to willingly make mistakes, given the challenges provided by the exercises, you should be able to focus on issues of graphic support and design strategies and allow the CAD software to teach itself.

Rather than learn how to draft in 2D CAD, it makes more sense to me to tackle 3D CAD immediately. By consistently exporting a variety of projections of 3D assignments into 2D for further modifications and plotting, students can establish their pattern of 3D-to-2D graphics.

Index

About the Author

Stephen Paul Jacobs is a professor at the School of
Architecture, Tulane University, teaching courses in
architectural design, theory, and CAD. He is a practicing
architect and a member of the Society of Architectural
Historians and the National Council of Returned Peace
Corps Volunteers. He was a Senior Fulbright Lecturer in
Bogotá, Columbia, and a Scholar in Residence at the
American Academy in Rome.